■ SCHOLASTIC

D0128633

TEACHING VOCABULARY
Differentiated Instruction With
Leveled Graphic Organizers

NANCY L. WITHERELL & MARY C. McMACKIN

NEW YORK • TORONTO • LONDON • AUCKLAND • SYDNEY
MEXICO CITY • NEW DELHI • HONG KONG • BUENOS AIRES

Teaching *Resources*

This book is dedicated to our editor, Sarah Longhi,
as she continues to guide and support us in our writing.

Editor: Sarah Longhi
Cover design by Maria Lilja
Interior design by Sydney Wright
Illustrations, pages 41 and 53 by Maxie Chambliss
ISBN-13 978-0-545-05900-8
ISBN-10 0-545-05900-3

1 2 3 4 5 6 7 8 9 10   40   15 14 13 12 11 10 09

Contents

Introduction

Imagine you are invited into a second-grade classroom to observe a vocabulary lesson. As you enter the room, you sense the excitement of children sitting on the floor near an easel. The teacher takes the big book she has just read off the easel and replaces it with a sheet of chart paper. The word *antonyms* is written in large, bold, red marker at the top of the chart paper. Down the side of the paper are seven words from the book the teacher has just read aloud. The teacher begins by explaining that *antonym* means *opposite*. She has prepared an interactive lesson to teach this concept and engages the students in identifying pictures she's prepared that show the words represented and their antonyms, and then in role-playing feeling words that are antonyms (*happy* and *sad*, *worried* and *calm*). At the end of the lesson, the children are ready to work independently with antonyms. The teacher passes out a graphic organizer to each student. Once the students begin to work, you circulate around the room and notice that there are three different graphic organizers being used. Looking over the students' shoulders, you see that all the organizers look equally demanding, but that there are slight differences in what the children are doing. You realize that this teacher has used tiered (leveled) graphic organizers to differentiate vocabulary instruction.

Differentiated Instruction

Tomlinson (1999) explains that teachers can modify three basic areas: content, process, and product. When we differentiate by using leveled graphic organizers, we are modifying products.

When we introduce a skill to a whole class (or even a subset of a class), the children in the group are not likely to learn at the same rate.

Some will catch on to the skill faster than others and some will be able to demonstrate their understanding in more complex ways than others. In order for all children to learn at an optimal pace, we match children with a reinforcing activity that allows each one to be successful at a cognitively appropriate level. For example, a teacher provides whole-class instruction on nouns, teaching students that nouns are the names of people, places, and things. After a lesson in which students learn the meanings of several teacher-selected nouns, students work independently on an activity that reinforces and extends what they've learned. Several students work on graphic organizers in which they draw pictures to go with the pre-taught nouns and label all other nouns in their pictures. Several other students work on graphic organizers that ask them to determine if the pre-taught nouns are names of people, places, or things, and then explain what each noun means. The remaining students work on graphic organizers that have them consider more deeply each word's meanings and in what contexts the words might be used.

At all three levels, students are using the leveled graphic organizers to reinforce the concept of *noun* and the meanings of the specific nouns their teacher introduced to the entire group. Each student feels successful because he or she is matched to an appropriate graphic organizer—one that is neither too easy nor too difficult.

Why Use Tiered Graphic Organizers?

In order to meet the diverse needs of students in today's classrooms, teachers must be able to design lessons that (1) meet individual instructional requirements, (2) stay within the curriculum, and (3) ensure consistent outcomes for all students. The use of tiered graphic organizers can help achieve the instructional goals.

Organizers are provided on three levels: a *beginning* level where students demonstrate a basic understanding of the target concept using pictures and a limited amount of writing; a *developing* level that is applicable for students who are ready to engage (with some support) in higher levels of thinking and more writing; and an *extending* level that is appropriate for students who are able to work (with limited support) on material that is more cognitively advanced than the lower two levels. Leveled graphic organizers make it possible for teachers to match each student with developmentally appropriate vocabulary activities while focusing on one overarching outcome for all students.

Although each graphic organizer fosters a different type and amount of thinking, the organizers look equally demanding and appealing. It's important to note that graphic organizers are not end products; rather, they are planners that students use to record ideas for a subsequent activity. In the primary grades, students might work on individual organizers and then share their ideas orally in a whole-class discussion. Other times, students might use the organizers as planning tools for writing activities. In all cases, the organizers should be viewed as a means to an end, not a final product.

Building Concepts for Primary Students

The report of the National Reading Panel (National Institute of Child Health and Human Development, 2000) identified vocabulary as one of five important areas in reading embraced by the No Child Left Behind Act of 2001. Paris (2005) states that of these five areas, vocabulary

and comprehension are considered *unconstrained* because we continue to grow in these two areas over our lifetime. But with so many words to learn, how do teachers determine what words to teach?

This book draws on research and practices established by Beck, McKeown, and Kucan (2002). They discuss three tiers that teachers can use to classify vocabulary words. Tier 1 words are common, everyday words that most primary students know and use regularly in their speaking and writing, such as *table, run, little,* and *fast.* Tier 2 words are more sophisticated words, not encountered everyday, but used often, such as *pretend, favorite, impossible,* and *noticed.* Tier 3 words are utilized less frequently in text, but are words students should know. These words are usually found in content-area materials. Words such as *mammal, habitats, liquid,* and *island* are Tier 3 words.

Generally, in primary-level classes, Tier 1 words need little reinforcement for meaning, but students may need a number of exposures to these words to build recognition. Tier 2 words should be purposefully taught and reinforced, and may be unfamiliar to students. Tier 2 words are important to students' academic success. Tier 3 words, too, are important as they enhance knowledge and provide students with specific content words. For example, when teaching the life cycle of a butterfly, *metamorphosis* may seem too difficult of a word for this level but is necessary for content comprehension.

Teaching Vocabulary: Differentiated Instruction With Leveled Graphic Organizers addresses the developmental needs and interests of primary-grade children. It emphasizes the need to build (as opposed to reinforce) concepts. Building a thorough understanding of literary concepts in the primary grades is crucial. These understandings form a foundation for a deeper development in the intermediate grades and beyond. The lessons cover key language-building concepts that enable you to introduce new words and reinforce the vocabulary words you've selected for students throughout the day and across the curriculum.

How Is This Book Organized?

Each chapter follows the same organizational structure:

- Names and defines a target concept

- Provides an activity to use with students through which the concept is introduced

- Transitions from a concrete activity to a piece of quality literature to illustrate the concept in a more abstract form

- Offers a model lesson in which direct instruction of the concept is provided that prepares students for the tiered graphic organizers

- Includes three tiered graphic organizers: beginning, developing, and extending

- Lists several picture books and one chapter book, with annotations, to use in follow-up lessons

The chapters in *Teaching Vocabulary: Differentiated Instruction With Leveled Graphic Organizers* may be used as stand-alone chapters, introduced in any order that meets your needs and those of your students. The chapters can also be introduced as units of study that build on one another. For example, it might make sense to introduce the chapter on synonyms before you teach antonyms. In addition, the vocabulary lessons and activities in this book can easily be incorporated into guided reading lessons or used in conjunction with basal reading series—you and your students choose the words they will learn.

Is This a Workbook?

No. This is not a vocabulary workbook, even though some workbooks can be useful for some students. Workbooks are texts that can be used one time—once the answers have been recorded on a page, the workbook has served its purpose. Conversely, the activities in this book are open-ended and may be used over and over again as your students grow and develop.

The tiered graphic organizers in this book were created to help you meet the needs of all learners as their knowledge of vocabulary grows. We hope you will find that differentiating learning with tiered graphic organizers is a useful tool in your classroom.

Sources Cited

Beck, I., McKeown, M., & Kucan, L. (2002). *Bringing words to life: Robust vocabulary instruction*. NY: Guilford.

Graves, M.F. (2006). *The vocabulary book: Learning and instruction*. Newark, DE: IRA.

National Institute of Child Health and Human Development. (2000). *Report of the National Reading Panel. Teaching children to read: An evidence-based assessment of the scientific research literature on reading and its implications for reading instruction* (NIH Publication No. 00-4769). Washington, DC.

Paris, S. (2005). Reinterpreting the development of reading skills. *Reading Research Quarterly*, 40, 184–202.

Tomlinson, C.A. (1999). *The differentiated classroom: Responding to the needs of all learners*. Alexandria, VA: ASCD.

White, T.G., Sowell, J., & Yanagihara, A. (1989). Teaching elementary students to use word-part clues. *The Reading Teacher*, 42(4), 302–308.

Learning New Words

Skill: *Recognize new words in print to deepen understanding of text.*

Description

It is important that students be exposed to words that they do not recognize in print or that may not be in their oral vocabulary. Students build a stronger vocabulary by regular introduction of new words in the context of read-aloud passages and shared reading and review of the words in multiple contexts.

Getting to Know the Concept

To help students gain ownership of new vocabulary words, follow a six- or eight-step introduction. The number of steps depends on how familiar readers are with the word. For instance, if students are learning to recognize a word in print that is already in their oral vocabulary, such as the word *table*, six steps are usually sufficient. If students are learning a word with an unfamiliar meaning, such as *cot* (a decodable word that is not frequently used), eight steps are often needed. Word meanings should then be reinforced through reinforcement activities provided on the graphic organizers.

Teaching the Concept With Literature

Books chosen to be read aloud should contain vocabulary that is approximately one year above students' reading levels to ensure that students are exposed to new words. Select new words from your read-aloud texts that are important to the content of the passage and that aid in students' comprehension.

The Six- or Eight-Step Method for Teaching New Words

Step 1 Display a simple sentence that contains the underlined new word. Read the sentence aloud, skipping the new word, as in a cloze procedure.

Step 2 Ask students if they can pronounce the word or figure out the word from what the sentence is saying. Make sure students use the correct pronunciation.

Step 3 Discuss the meaning of the new word. Write the word on the front of a word card and the definition on the back (prepare in advance).

Step 4 Using the word card, discuss the word shape, its similarity to any other words students know, and any other features that will help them recognize the new word.

Step 5 Have a student match the word card with the word in the sentence.

Step 6 Together as a group, reread the sentence containing the new word.

(Continue with the following steps for teaching words with unknown meanings.)

Step 7 Ask students to repeat the word's meaning. Show the definition on the back of the word card.

Step 8 Have students say a sentence to a partner using the new word or have volunteers say a sentence to the group.

Model Lesson

Choose a book with about five new words, such as *There's a Hole in My Pocket* (Gibson, 1994). This simple story is based on a traditional American song. Five possible words are *hole, pocket, sew, needle, thread.*

Step 1 Show the word *needle* in a sentence, with *needle* underlined.

My mother used a <u>needle</u> to sew my pants.

Read the sentence, skipping the word *needle*. Say "blank" in the word's place.

Step 2 Ask students if they can say the word. Make sure they use correct pronunciation.

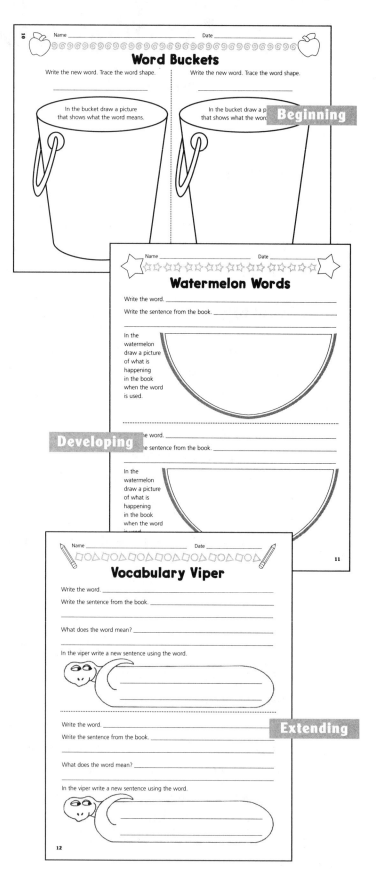

Step 3 Discuss the meaning of the word *needle*. Show a picture or draw one. Have students describe how a needle is used. Write *needle* on a word card. Write "a sharp pin with a hole in one end used for sewing" on the back of the card (prepare in advance).

Step 4 Using the word card, discuss the shape of the word. Show how it has high letters toward the end. Ask students if they see a familiar word in the word *needle*? Cover, or have a volunteer cover, the "le" and show the word *need*.

Step 5 Have a student match the *needle* word card with the word *needle* in the sentence.

Step 6 Together as a group, reread the sentence containing the word *needle*.

Use Steps 7 and 8 if students could not provide the meaning in Step 3 or did not seem familiar enough with the meaning.

Step 7 Ask students to tell again what *needle* means. Show the definition on the card.

Step 8 Have students say a sentence to a partner using the word *needle*.

For additional practice, have each student complete an organizer at his or her skill level.

Graphic Organizers

Beginning: **Word Buckets** (page 10)
Students write the word, trace its shape, and draw a picture representing the word meaning.

Developing: **Watermelon Words** (page 11)
Students write the word, write the sentence from the book, and draw a picture that shows how the word is used in the book.

Extending: **Vocabulary Viper** (page 12)
Students write the word, write the sentence from the book, write what the word means, and write a new sentence using the word.

Great Books for This Activity

Picture Books

Gibson, A. (1994). *There's a hole in my pocket.* New York: Scholastic

James, H. F. (2007). *S is for s'mores.* Chelsea, MI: Sleeping Bear Press.

Trivizas, E. (1994). *The three little wolves and the big bad pig.* New York: Scholastic.

Chapter Book

Star, N. (2006). *Case of the April fool's frogs.* New York: Scholastic.

Word Buckets

Write the new word. Trace the word shape.

In the bucket draw a picture that shows what the word means.

Write the new word. Trace the word shape.

In the bucket draw a picture that shows what the word means.

Watermelon Words

Write the word. _____

Write the sentence from the book. _____

_____

In the watermelon draw a picture of what is happening in the book when the word is used.

Write the word. _____

Write the sentence from the book. _____

_____

In the watermelon draw a picture of what is happening in the book when the word is used.

11

Vocabulary Viper

Write the word. _____

Write the sentence from the book. _____

_____

What does the word mean? _____

_____

In the viper write a new sentence using the word.

_____

Write the word. _____

Write the sentence from the book. _____

_____

What does the word mean? _____

_____

In the viper write a new sentence using the word.

Multiple-Meaning Words

Skill: *Recognize that words can have more than one meaning.*

Description

The word *down* can mean to move in a lower direction, to consume something (*Sam downed three hamburgers.*), to be sick (*Crystal has come down with the flu.*), a football designation (*"First down!" yelled the referee.*), or soft feathers (*Eva wore a down jacket to keep warm.*). Each meaning is dependent upon the context in which the word is used—a concept that may be new and confusing for students. In order to help them comprehend texts, especially content-area texts where common words often take on content-specific meanings, students need to be aware that words can have different meanings.

Getting to Know the Concept

Begin instruction on multiple-meaning words by focusing on one word, such as *tie*. Display a sneaker with laces to tie, a man's tie (necktie), and a scoreboard with a soccer score of 3–3 (tie score). Talk with students about the word *tie* and how one word can have different meanings. If needed, repeat with the word *check*. Conclude by pointing out that, when reading, if one meaning doesn't make sense, good readers try to determine if another meaning is possible.

Teaching the Concept With Literature

Children's literature is filled with multiple-meaning words. Point out any multiple-meaning words you find in your current read-aloud book. Have students share various definitions for these words. Explain that good readers know that some words have more than one meaning. When they come across a word that doesn't make sense, they consider other definitions or recognize that there might be other possible definitions, and continue to read with this understanding in mind.

Model Lesson

Choose a book with several multiple-meaning words, such as *And If the Moon Could Talk* (Banks, 1998). This quiet tale tells what the moon would say as it looks down on Earth. Reread the book, pausing at multiple-meaning words, such as *lies, light, stars, waves, crab, safe, hands, den*.

For each word, create a table that has several columns and rows (see below). In the first column, write the target word. In the second column, write the sentence in which the word appears. Write a different meaning for the word in each successive column.

Below each definition, encourage students to make associations. Ask: "What do you think of when you hear this word being used in this particular way?" Making associations for each meaning will help students consider the word from different perspectives.

Continue in this same way for other multiple-meaning words in the book. Remind students that they often come across multiple-meaning words while reading and that clues around the multiple-meaning words will help them figure out the appropriate meaning.

For additional practice, have each student complete an organizer at his or her skill level.

Graphic Organizers

Beginning: **Marvelous Meanings** (page 16)
Provide a sentence that contains a multiple-meaning word for students to write (or write a sentence on the graphic organizer before photocopying it). Students copy the target word and draw a picture of what the word means in this sentence. Students determine a second meaning for the target word and draw another picture to illustrate this meaning.

Developing: **Meeting Many Meanings** (page 17)
Provide a sentence that contains a multiple-meaning word for students to write (or write a sentence on the graphic organizer before photocopying it). Students copy the target word, write two meanings for the word, and make associations (i.e., what they think of when they hear the word used in this way). Students repeat this process with a second multiple-meaning word.

Word	Sentence	1st meaning	2nd meaning	3rd meaning
lies	Somewhere a pair of shoes lies under a chair.	to be placed in a certain spot	to say something that isn't true	
		What do you think of when you hear this meaning?		
		My dog lies on a rug. Dad lies down when he feels tired.	A child lies about eating candy. It is bad to tell lies.	

Extending: **More Than One Meaning**

(page 18)

Provide students with one multiple-meaning word from a text they are reading. Students write the word, three different meanings, and make associations for each meaning. They repeat the activity using a multiple-meaning word they find in a text they are reading.

Great Books for This Activity

Picture Books

Banks, K. (1998). *And if the moon could talk.* New York: Farrar, Straus and Giroux. (Multiple-meaning words include: *lies, light, stars, waves, crab, safe, hands, den.*)

Cronin, D. (2000). *Click, clack, moo: Cows that type.* New York: Simon & Schuster. (Multiple-meaning words include: *type, strike, note, left, farm, party.*)

Pitzer, S. (2006). *Not afraid of dogs.* New York: Walker & Company. (Multiple-meaning words include: *saw, left, honey, crack, safe.*)

Chapter Book

Guest, E. H. (2003). *Iris and Walter and Cousin Howie.* San Diego: Harcourt. (Multiple-meaning words include: *fish, show, hopped, warm up, catch.*)

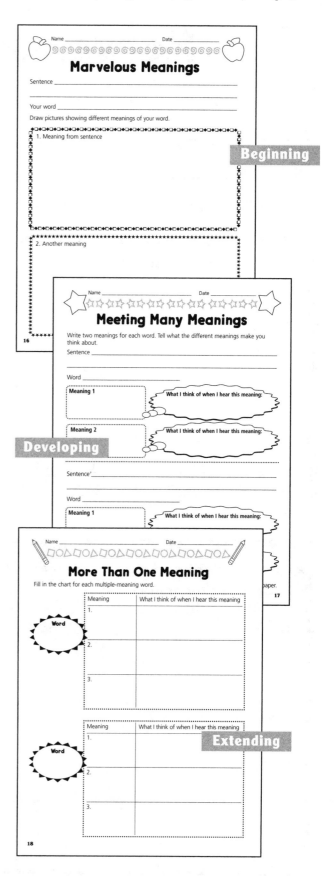

Name _____   Date _____

Marvelous Meanings

Sentence _____

_____

Your word _____

Draw pictures showing different meanings of your word.

1. Meaning from sentence

2. Another meaning

Meeting Many Meanings

Write two meanings for each word. Tell what the different meanings make you think about.

Sentence _____

_____

Word _____

Meaning 1

What I think of when I hear this meaning:

Meaning 2

What I think of when I hear this meaning:

Sentence _____

_____

Word _____

Meaning 1

What I think of when I hear this meaning:

Meaning 2

What I think of when I hear this meaning:

If you think of other meanings for these words, write them on the back of this paper.

More Than One Meaning

Fill in the chart for each multiple-meaning word.

Meaning	What I think of when I hear this meaning
1.	
2.	
3.	

Word

Meaning	What I think of when I hear this meaning
1.	
2.	
3.	

Word

Nouns

Skill: *Acquire new vocabulary that represents people, places, and things.*

Description

Because children encounter nouns everywhere in their daily lives, we can use their experiences to introduce and reinforce new vocabulary words. Although we may think of nouns as basic elements of the English language, they can be confusing for English language learners, especially for children who are used to assigning a gender to nouns (e.g., Spanish, French, and Portuguese). Since most nouns represent tangible objects, there are often concrete examples or at least pictures that make nouns comprehensible and accessible for all learners.

Getting to Know the Concept

Introduce nouns with riddles and noun searches. Put a plastic spoon, a toy, a piece of fruit, an object from your classroom (e.g., crayon), or a picture of a person or place into a brown paper bag. Students should not be able to see the object. Give one simple clue about the object. For example, if the bag contains a picture of a playground, you might say, "Children like to go there to ride on swings." Have students guess. If nobody guesses correctly, give another clue. Continue until students guess correctly. Then, show the object to students and write its name on chart paper. Repeat the process with other objects giving one clue at a time, having students guess, and recording the name of the object on chart paper. When you have made a list of five or six words, help students deduce that all the words name people, places, and things. Explain that the words are nouns. Point out other nouns in the room and invite students to identify nouns they see. Add the nouns to the word list.

Take students to the gym, cafeteria, nurse's office, and school bus. Have them find several nouns in each location and record them in their notebooks. When you return to the classroom, talk about any nouns they listed that go beyond the basic vocabulary they use regularly in their oral language. These Tier 2 words (see page 5) are more sophisticated words that are used across disciplines (e.g., *equipment, cash register, thermometer, aisle*). Remind students that knowing the names of people, places, and things will help them express ideas and understand what they read.

Teaching the Concept With Literature

After students have had opportunities to identify familiar nouns, move to a more abstract activity, using books. Choose a riddle book that provides clues and pictures of objects, such as *What Am I? Very First Riddles* (Calmenson, 1989). As you read each description, stop and have students guess, draw, or write the noun. After reading the book, review any nouns that are Tier 2 words for your students. Extend the activity and provide additional Tier 2 words by creating riddles that go with pictures from magazines.

Model Lesson

Introduce (or review) nouns by having available a big book that the students know well. Choose a book that contains simple, clear pictures of people, places, and things, such as *If You Take a Mouse to School* (Numeroff, 2002). Identify Tier 2 nouns in the first page of the book and list them on chart paper. Then, go on a "picture walk" through three or four more pages of the book and help students identify several other Tier 2 nouns in the pictures. Add the nouns to the list on the chart paper. Clarify the meaning of each noun by providing a definition, an association, an example, or a synonym for each word. Brainstorm where you might

see this noun in the environment.

Model categorizing nouns by writing the appropriate word—*person, place,* or *thing*—after each noun in the list. Some nouns might fit into more than one category. The beginning of your chart might look like the one below. There will be about 15 nouns on the completed chart.

Bring closure to the lesson by having volunteers give a definition for a noun. Have students offer examples of each category of nouns. Explain that knowing the meaning of nouns helps us understand what we read and that using specific nouns helps us express ourselves clearly.

For additional practice, have each student complete an organizer at his or her skill level.

Graphic Organizers

Beginning: **Nifty Nouns** (page 22)
Using two teacher-assigned nouns, students draw a picture of each in the setting where they would likely see it. They label the target noun and all other nouns in each picture.

Noun	What does the noun mean?	Where would you see it?
faucet (thing)	a pipe that water travels through	kitchen, bathroom
drainer (thing)	a rack where people place wet dishes to dry	on the counter near the kitchen sink
blender (thing)	a machine that chops food	kitchen
classmates (people)	children in the class—like Rayna, Evan, and Bettina	school, playground, after-school activities
science laboratory (place)	a place where scientists do experiments	high school, college, where scientists work

Developing: **A Nose for Nouns** (page 23)
Using four teacher-assigned nouns, students list the words. They identify whether each noun is a person, place, or thing and write the meaning for each.

Extending: **Noun News!** (page 24)
Using three teacher-assigned nouns, students list the words. They identify each one as a person, place, or thing, write each meaning, and list where they might see the noun in the environment.

Great Books for This Activity

Picture Books

Calmenson, S. (1989). *What am I? Very first riddles.* New York: Scholastic.

Freeman, D. (1978). *A pocket for Corduroy.* New York: Viking. (Nouns include: *laundry, towels, washcloths, beret, overalls, studio, manager, mountainside, señorita, rascal.*)

Numeroff, L. (2002). *If you take a mouse to school.* New York: Laura Geringer.

Zolotow, C. (1984). *I know a lady.* New York: Puffin. (Nouns include: *block, lady, garden, daffodils, spring, zinnias, summer, chrysanthemums, fall, snow, Halloween, meadow.*)

Chapter Book

Kline, S. (2006). *Herbie Jones sails into second grade.* New York: Putnam. (Nouns include: *ingredients, cupboard, scoops, expressions, gutter, shadow, anchor, footsteps, scarf, voyage, microphone, operator.*)

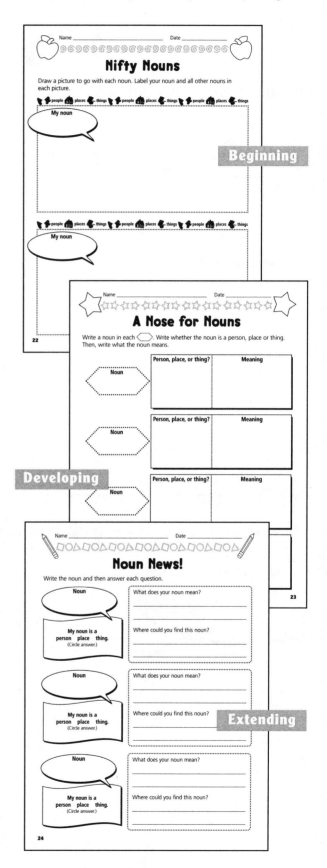

Nifty Nouns

Draw a picture to go with each noun. Label your noun and all other nouns in each picture.

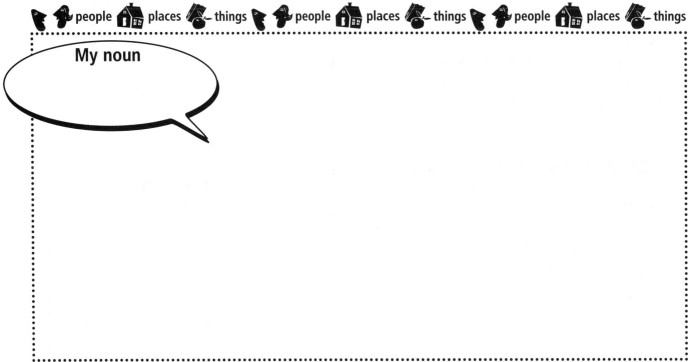

A Nose for Nouns

Write a noun in each ⬡. Write whether the noun is a person, place or thing.
Then, write what the noun means.

Noun

Person, place, or thing?	Meaning

Noun

Person, place, or thing?	Meaning

Noun

Person, place, or thing?	Meaning

Noun

Person, place, or thing?	Meaning

Noun News!

Write the noun and then answer each question.

Noun

My noun is a
person   place   thing.
(Circle answer.)

What does your noun mean?

_____

_____

Where could you find this noun?

_____

_____

Noun

My noun is a
person   place   thing.
(Circle answer.)

What does your noun mean?

_____

_____

Where could you find this noun?

_____

_____

Noun

My noun is a
person   place   thing.
(Circle answer.)

What does your noun mean?

_____

_____

Where could you find this noun?

_____

_____

Verbs

Skill: *Enhance oral and written vocabulary by using strong verbs.*

Description

For primary-grade students, verbs are defined as action words. All sentences contain verbs and most can be demonstrated or acted out. Students can enhance their speaking and written vocabulary by focusing on strong verbs when they listen and read.

Getting to Know the Concept

Since verbs are action words, what better way to learn about verbs than to move around? Start by making a set of flashcards with a verb on each one. Depending on the grade you teach, you might use words such as *hop, skip, dance, clap, whisper, tap, bow, groan, wink, invite,* and *scrub.* Have students perform or mime the action associated with each verb. Remind students that verbs show actions, even small actions that we barely notice, such as *stare, stand,* and *breathe.*

Teaching the Concept With Literature

Introduce verbs with a book of photographs, such as *What Dogs Do* (Beals, 1995). Each two-page spread in this small book contains a verb and a photograph of a dog that exemplifies the verb. Explain that the author used strong verbs. You may wish to display a photograph and have students come up with their own verbs and then compare them to Beals' text. Beals uses verbs such as *endure, ponder, hope, wag, wait,* and *pretend.*

Model Lesson

Choose a read-aloud with strong verbs that your students can perform, such as *Brave Irene* (Steig, 1986). This story tells about the night Irene forges through wind and snow to deliver a ball gown. After reading and enjoying the book, list eight or nine verbs from the text that are new vocabulary words for your students. The words should be Tier 2 words (page 5), such as *admit, insist, add, cover, slip, whirl, hurry, stumble,* and *caution.* Since the past tense of verbs are used in *Brave Irene,* record the base word and the past tense on a T-chart, noting the difference. (When teaching the vocabulary, focus on the base word.)

Select two words from the original list of eight or nine verbs. Have a student perform the action represented by one of the verbs. Write the verb on chart paper. Next, write a sentence that describes the student's action, being sure to include the target vocabulary word. Have another student perform the second verb. Ask the student to write the verb on the chart paper. With students, brainstorm a sentence to describe the student's action. Write it on the chart paper.

Prepare a three-column chart (see below) and list the two verbs in the left column. Model a think-aloud as to who might perform the action and record your answer in the middle column of the chart. Model completing the third column by stating when the action would be performed. Discussing who might use the verbs and when the person might perform the action places the verbs in contexts that help students retain the words' meanings. Repeat the procedure with the second verb.

Conclude the lesson by reminding students that verbs are used to show specific actions. Invite them to be on the lookout for interesting verbs throughout each day and encourage them to use their new vocabulary when speaking and writing.

For additional practice, have each student complete an organizer at his or her skill level.

Graphic Organizers

Beginning: **Ready, Set, Go!** (page 28)
Using two teacher-assigned verbs, students draw pictures depicting someone or something performing the action associated with each verb. Students write the verb next to the corresponding action in each picture.

Developing: **Lights, Camera, Action!** (page 29)
Students list five or six teacher-assigned verbs. They select two that show actions they can do or would like to do and draw pictures depicting each of the two actions. Then they write a sentence for each picture that uses the target verb.

Extending: **Verbs in Action** (page 30)
Students list up to eight verbs, identify who or what might perform each action, and tell when this person/animal might perform the action.

Verb	Who might do this?	When would the person do this?
admit	a little girl	Tara will admit that she ate the cookies.
stumble	a man carrying groceries	He might stumble and fall if he can't see where he is walking.

Great Books for This Activity

Picture Books

Beals, S. (1995). *What dogs do*. San Francisco: Chronicle Books.

de Beer, H. (1999). *Little polar bear*. New York: North-South Books. (Verbs include: *covered, showed, disappeared, reappeared, drifted, burned, surrounded*.)

Fox, M. (1989). *Night noises*. San Diego: Harcourt Brace Jovanovich. (Verbs include: *raced, dozed, banged, rattled, cocked, bristled, whispered, peeped, rumpled*.)

Steig, W. (1986). *Brave Irene*. New York: Farrar, Straus, Giroux.

Chapter Book

Giff, P. R. (1992). *The secret at the Polk Street School*. New York: Delacorte. (Verbs include: *kneeling, poking, smoothed, disappeared, marched, blinked, crawled*.)

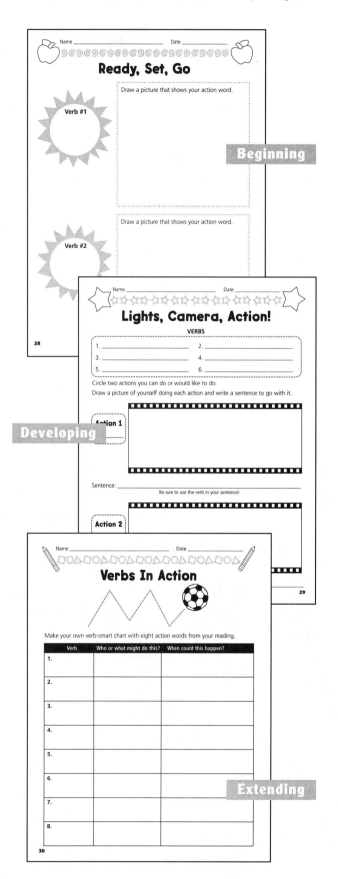

Name _____ Date _____

Ready, Set, Go

Verb #1

Draw a picture that shows your action word.

Beginning

Verb #2

Draw a picture that shows your action word.

28

Name _____ Date _____

Lights, Camera, Action!

VERBS

1. _____ 2. _____
3. _____ 4. _____
5. _____ 6. _____

Circle two actions you can do or would like to do.
Draw a picture of yourself doing each action and write a sentence to go with it.

Developing

Action 1

Sentence: _____
Be sure to use the verb in your sentence!

Action 2

29

Name _____ Date _____

Verbs In Action

Make your own verb-smart chart with eight action words from your reading.

Verb	Who or what might do this?	When could this happen?
1.		
2.		
3.		
4.		
5.		
6.		
7.		
8.		

Extending

30

Ready, Set, Go

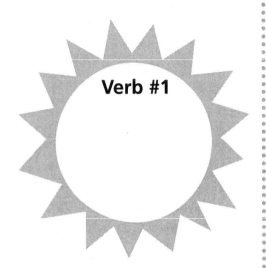

Verb #1

Draw a picture that shows your action word.

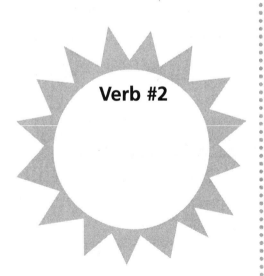

Verb #2

Draw a picture that shows your action word.

Lights, Camera, Action!

VERBS

1. _____ 2. _____

3. _____ 4. _____

5. _____ 6. _____

Circle two actions you can do or would like to do.

Draw a picture of yourself doing each action and write a sentence to go with it.

Action 1
_____

Sentence: _____

Be sure to use the verb in your sentence!

Action 2
_____

Sentence: _____

Verbs In Action

Make your own verb-smart chart with eight action words from your reading.

Verb	Who or what might do this?	When could this happen?
1.		
2.		
3.		
4.		
5.		
6.		
7.		
8.		

Adjectives

Skill: *Increase the number of describing words used in oral and written language.*

Description

Adjectives give information about the nouns or pronouns they describe—for example, a *cranky* boy, a *forgetful* elephant, and a *magical* castle. In each case, the adjective helps the reader picture the noun. What happens if we change only the adjectives? We might have a *frightened* boy, a *thirsty* elephant, and a *haunted* castle. Our mental images change significantly. How we envision people, places, and things often depends on the adjectives we use to describe them. When students have a rich array of adjectives at their fingertips, the adjectives can be used to add details to their speaking and writing. In addition, students use their knowledge of adjectives to fully comprehend a writer's message.

Getting to Know the Concept

Label objects in your classroom, such as the door, window, cubby, sink, desk, and rug. Next, cut strips of colored construction paper or oak tag. On each strip, write one word that describes each noun. For example, you might write *wooden* to go with *door*, *cracked* (window), *organized* (cubby), *soapy* (sink), *cluttered* (desk), *paint-stained* (rug). Tape each adjective beside the noun it describes. Help students realize that the adjectives provide information about the objects.

On more strips, write one additional word that describes each object. For example, *squeaky* (door), *streaky* (window), *yellow* (cubby), *wet* (sink), *messy* (desk), *square* (rug). Shuffle the strips and read aloud the word on the first strip. Have a student put the word with the object it describes. Continue to match words and objects until each object has two descriptive words. Explain that the descriptive words are adjectives. Finally, have students brainstorm an additional adjective for each object. Record their adjectives on the strips. Attach each new adjective to the noun it describes and discuss how it gives additional information about the noun.

Teaching the Concept With Literature

Choose a book where students can mix and match pictures of people, animals, or things, such as *The Mix and Match Book of Dinosaurs* (Sanders, 1992). Have a volunteer arrange the pages of the book to create a unique creature. Model describing this creature. For example, "This creature has a curved tail, a spiked body, and a horned head." Have students make and describe their own creatures. Guide them to see that the adjectives they use are describing words that help us picture people, places, and things.

Model Lesson

Choose a book that has many descriptive adjectives, such as *Time for Ballet* (Geras, 2003). This is the story of a young girl going to ballet class, practicing, and even overcoming pre-performance jitters. Read aloud the book, focusing on key nouns and adjectives. For example, Tilly says that Tuesdays are her favorite day of the week. Write *favorite* in the first column of a four-column chart. Write day in the second column. As you continue reading, ask students to identify nouns and adjectives. Fill in the first two columns of the chart. After you have a few adjectives and nouns on your chart, go back and model completing the third and fourth columns.

As you continue through the book, point out unconventional adjectives, such as "a *leapy* cat" or "a *curled-up-to-sleepy* cat." Talk about the purpose adjectives serve (to give readers information about the noun).

Divide students into small groups. Give each group an object to describe. Encourage them to come up with creative adjectives to describe the object. Add the new adjectives to your chart. By using these creative adjectives, you and your students can have fun with language and reinforce how adjectives paint pictures of nouns in our minds.

For additional practice, have each student complete an organizer at his or her skill level.

Graphic Organizers

Beginning: **Adjective Artist** (page 34)
Using two teacher-assigned adjectives, students draw an object that has the feature their chosen adjective describes. They also write each adjective and the noun it describes.

Developing: **All About Adjectives** (page 35)
Students define three adjectives from the lesson. They also list other nouns they can use the adjective to describe.

Extending: **Adjectives Anyone?** (page 36)
Students give a synonym for three adjectives from the lesson, tell other nouns each can describe, and create a unique adjective to describe an object in the classroom.

Adjective	Noun	What does the adjective mean?	Other nouns the adjective could describe?
favorite	day	liked the best	pet, friend, food
pretty	leotard and tutu	beautiful	Mom, dress, flower
pink	leotard and tutu	light red color	backpack, bike
purple	leotard	reddish-blue color	jacket, popsicle, juice

Great Books for This Activity

Picture Books

Fleming, D. (2001). *Pumpkin eye*. New York: Henry Holt and Company. (Adjectives include: *yellow* moon, *pumpkin* eye, *burning* wicks, and *pounding* feet.)

Geras, A. (2003). *Time for ballet*. New York: Dial.

Sanders, G. (1992). *The mix and match book of dinosaurs*. New York: Simon & Schuster.

Staake, B. (2006). *The red lemon*. New York: Golden Books. (Adjectives include: *blue* sea; lemons that are *mellow, tangy, tasty, tart,* and *yellow*; *sweet birthday* cakes; *fresh fruity* shakes; *once-yellow* and *crimson* cupcakes.)

Chapter Book

Adler, D.A. (1984). *Cam Jansen and the mystery of the monster movie*. New York: Puffin. (Adjectives include: *ordinary* people; *light* snow; *second* poster; *swinging* doors; *four empty* seats; *dark, blank* screen.)

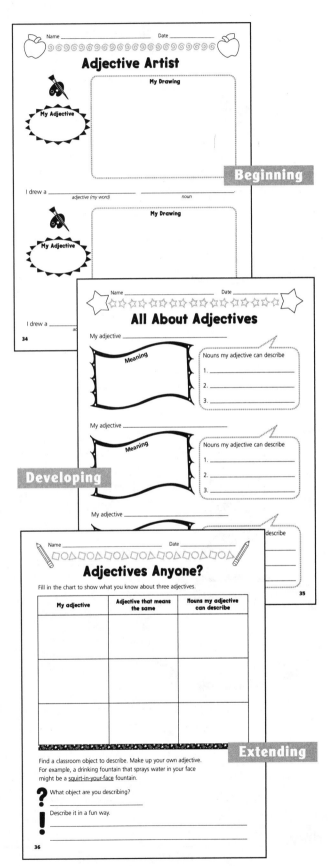

Adjective Artist

My Adjective

My Drawing

I drew a _____ _____.
adjective (my word)   *noun*

My Adjective

My Drawing

I drew a _____ _____.
adjective (my word)   *noun*

All About Adjectives

My adjective _____

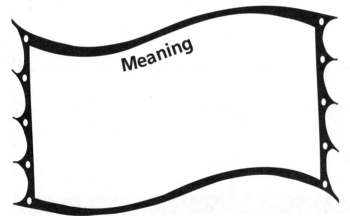

Meaning

Nouns my adjective can describe

1. _____

2. _____

3. _____

My adjective _____

Meaning

Nouns my adjective can describe

1. _____

2. _____

3. _____

My adjective _____

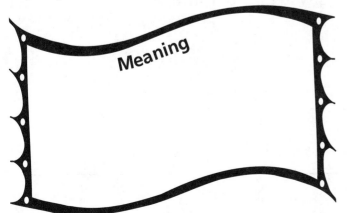

Meaning

Nouns my adjective can describe

1. _____

2. _____

3. _____

Adjectives Anyone?

Fill in the chart to show what you know about three adjectives.

My adjective	Adjective that means the same	Nouns my adjective can describe

Find a classroom object to describe. Make up your own adjective.
For example, a drinking fountain that sprays water in your face
might be a <u>squirt-in-your-face</u> fountain.

? What object are you describing?

_____

! Describe it in a fun way.

_____

_____

Rhyming Words

Skill: *Identify and match words that rhyme.*

Description

By definition, words that rhyme are words that end in the same sound. The ability to hear rhymes in words is valuable to beginning readers in two ways. First, it allows the reader to predict unknown words when the text offers a rhyming sequence. This supports both fluency and comprehension. Second, it helps readers identify particular spelling patterns and variant spellings of similar sounds. This aids in word recognition. Eventually the ability to rhyme words, in conjunction with understanding word meanings, allows readers to use analogy as a strategy to figure out unknown words.

Getting to Know the Concept

For most students, highlighting onset and rime on word walls, playing rhyming guessing games, and asking for rhyming words or "a word that sounds like . . ." will reinforce the identification of simple rhymes.

Begin instruction on rhyme by reviewing the meaning of *rhyme*. Use a verse students are familiar with such as "See you later, alligator" and "After a while, crocodile" or "Roses are red, violets are blue. Sugar is sweet and so are you." You might also share rhyming pictures, such as *dog/log, chair/hair, floor/door,* and *mat/hat.* Next, give students a practice rhyme-riddle to solve.

I rhyme with the word start. *When you draw you make me.* (art)

Then have students say the two rhyming words, *start/art.* Once students understand the riddle game, continue with the following riddles.

❀ I rhyme with the word *tar*. Your parents may drive me. (car)

❀ I rhyme with *knee* and I open a door. (key)

❀ I rhyme with *hook* and you read me. (book)

❀ I rhyme with *horn* and can begin with *pop*. (corn)

❀ I rhyme with *cape* and I'm sticky. (tape)

❀ I rhyme with *clip* and I'm a part of your body. (hip)

❀ I rhyme with *darker* and you can draw with me. (marker)

❀ I rhyme with *baboon* and you blow me up with air. (balloon)

❀ I rhyme with *commuter* and you play learning games on me. (computer)

Teaching the Concept With Literature

One of the great joys of teaching the primary grades is reading aloud all the creative and playful rhyming books written for this level. As you read books with rhyming lines, stop and let students use the meaning and rhyme together to deduce the word. When reading aloud poetry, whether in a big book, on a chart, or a smart board, take time to point to the rhyming words and show how they make sense in the poem.

Model Lesson

Choose a book with an engaging rhyme, such as *Silly Sally* (Wood, 1992). Silly Sally goes to town walking backwards upside down and meets silly animals on her silly journey. Begin by reading the book in its entirety, letting students get the feel for the rhyme. Reread the story, this time letting students provide the ending rhyme. Write the rhyming pairs on a chart, leaving space to add other words.

Once the chart is completed with rhyming pairs from the book, have students provide additional rhyming words for the *Words We Know* column. Together as a class read the rhyming words. Point out that not all rhyming words have the same spelling, but they do share the same sound. For each rhyme, ask students to pronounce the ending sound that makes the rhyme. Reinforce the list of rhyming words by making up rhyme riddles, such as "I rhyme with *down* and I am funny. (clown)"

For additional practice, have each student complete an organizer at his or her skill level.

Graphic Organizers

Beginning: **Rhyme Time** (page 40)
Students select three pairs of rhyming words from their book. They draw a picture of the rhyming words and write the word under each picture.

Developing: **The Bear Pair** (page 41)
Students list two rhyming pairs from their book. They list other words that rhyme with the pair.

In the book		Words we know
town	down	clown, gown, frown, brown
pig	jig	dig, wig, rig, twig
dog	leapfrog	log, bog, hog, clog
loon	tune	dune, moon, June
sheep	sleep	deep, peep, beep, leap
buttercup	up	pup, catsup, cup

Extending: **The Middle Riddle in the Dandy Candy** (page 42)

Students write a rhyming pair in one end of a candy wrapper. In the middle of the candy wrapper, they write a rhyme riddle using one of the words in the clue. The answer to the riddle is written in the other end of the candy wrapper.

Great Books for This Activity

Picture Books

Newman, L. (2004). *Where is bear?* Orlando, FL: Gulliver Books. Cute poem story about a bear who wants to sleep.

Shields, C.D. (2002). *The bugliest bug.* Cambridge, MA: Candlewick. This poem story has lots of great rhyming words to stretch vocabulary.

Wood, A. (1992). *Silly Sally.* San Diego: Harcourt.

Chapter Book

Newman, L. (2004). *The boy who cried fabulous.* Berkeley, CA: Tricycle Press. Although not a chapter book, this rhyming story is long enough to be one.

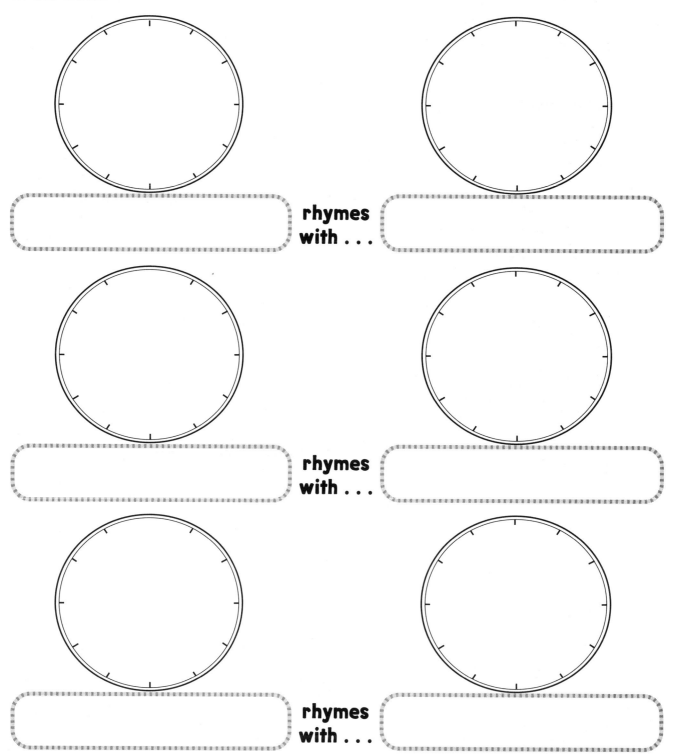

Rhyme Time

Write two rhyming words under the clock faces. Draw a picture of the word in the clock.

rhymes with . . .

rhymes with . . .

rhymes with . . .

The Bear Pair

On the bears' umbrella, write two words that rhyme. Beside the bears, write other words that rhyme with the bear pair.

_____

rhymes with . . .

_____

Other words that rhyme:

_____

_____

_____

_____

_____

rhymes with . . .

_____

Other words that rhyme:

_____

_____

_____

_____

41

The Middle Riddle in the Dandy Candy

Write a rhyming pair in the first part of the candy wrapper. In the middle, write a rhyme riddle using one of the words in the clue. Write the riddle answer in the far end of the wrapper.

Example:

Pair	Riddle	Answer
clown down	I rhyme with down and I am funny.	clown

Pair	Riddle	Answer
_____ _____	_____ _____	_____

Pair	Riddle	Answer
_____ _____	_____ _____	_____

Pair	Riddle	Answer
_____ _____	_____ _____	_____

Compound Words

Skill: *Determine the meanings of compound words by understanding their structure.*

Description

Compound words, such as *popcorn, bathtub, birthday, newspaper,* and *mailbox,* are made up of two (or more) individual words. Interestingly, some compound words, such as *firefighter,* are written as one single word (closed compounds), while similar compound words, such as *fire truck,* are written as two separate words (open compounds). In addition, some compound words have hyphens, such as *merry-go-round.*

Many students are intimidated when they attempt to read long, multi-syllabic words. Showing them that some long words are made up of two (or three) small words should enhance their self-confidence. In addition, the meaning of the two smaller words often provides insights into the meaning of the compound word (i.e., *sunscreen* or *toothpaste*). Investigating compound words provides students and teachers with opportunities to explore how our language works.

Compound Query

Why are some compound words written as a single word while others are separated into two words? Actually, there isn't a strict rule about how compound words are written. Since words in our language are formed and change forms for different purposes, check a dictionary if you are in doubt about whether a compound word is closed or open.

The following Scholastic Web site provides a list of compound words: **http://content.scholastic.com/content/ collateral_resources/pdf/r/reading_ bestpractices_vocabulary_compound_ words.pdf.**

Getting to Know the Concept

Start a collection of objects, photographs, or magazine pictures that represent compound words, such as *baseball, doorknob, earring, pillowcase,* and *tablecloth.* Have students identify each object. Write the name of each on chart paper. When the list is complete, read the list, pointing to each word as you go. Then ask students to determine what the words have in common. Students should notice that each word is made up of two smaller words.

Have volunteers circle the two small words in each compound word on the chart. (If students don't already know the term *compound words*, introduce it and provide a simple definition, such as "two or more smaller words that are combined into one word.") Talk about how readers often use the meanings of the two smaller words to determine the meaning of the compound word. Go back to the words on the list and have students test out this idea.

Teaching the Concept With Literature

To introduce this concept with literature, select a book that contains several compound words that can easily be defined by looking at the meaning of the two smaller words (e.g., *birthday*—the day of one's birth). Explain that good readers look for familiar words in long words. When they find an unfamiliar compound word, they can try to determine its meaning by using the two smaller words.

Model Lesson

Choose a book that has a title containing a compound word, such as *Iris and Walter: The Sleepover* (Guest, 2002). As you read the book, you'll notice the following compound words: *afternoon, suitcase, homesick, Grandpa, everybody, into,* and *everyone.* You'll also notice how the author uses *sleep over* (two words) and *sleepover* (one word) in different contexts: Compare "Iris was going to sleep over" to "It will be my first sleepover."

As you read, point out the compound words, write them on chart paper, have students come up and circle the two smaller words within each compound word, and talk about their meaning. Determine whether or not the two separate words were used to determine the meaning of the compound word. If so, write "yes" beside the compound word. Finally, explain that sometimes we can use the smaller words to make other compound words. For example, using the two smaller words in *sleepover*, we could make: *oversleep, sleepwalk, overboard, overcrowded, overfill, overnight, overstay, overhand.* If it seems appropriate, have students use a dictionary to find more compound words.

For additional practice, have each student complete an organizer at his or her skill level.

Graphic Organizers

Beginning: **Daydreaming About Compound Words** (page 46)
Given two teacher-selected compound words, students write the smaller words in each compound word. Then they draw a picture that shows what the compound word means.

Developing: **Stepping Up to Compound Words** (page 47)
Students locate a compound word in a text they are reading and write it on the top step of a ladder. They write the two small words contained in the compound on the rungs. They then draw and define the compound word and note whether or not they were able to use the meaning of the two smaller words to determine the meaning of the compound word.

Extending: **Fishing for Compound Words**
(page 48)

Students locate a compound word in a text they are reading and write it and its two small words in the fishbowl. Students define the compound word and then use the smaller words in the original compound word to brainstorm other compound words.

Great Books for This Activity

(Note: All these books have compound words in the title.)

Picture Books

Guest, E.H. (2002). *Iris and Walter, the sleepover.* San Diego: Harcourt, Inc.

Meddaugh, S. (1991). *The Witches' supermarket.* Boston: Houghton Mifflin. (Compounds include: *everybody, anyone, something, supermarket, inside, household, anymore, another.*)

Williams, B. (2003). *Albert's impossible toothache.* Cambridge, MA: Candlewick Press. (Compounds include: *toothache, toothless, bedroom, goodbye, blackberries, anything, outside, birthday, sleepover, into, grandmother, grandson, Disneyland.*)

Williams, V.B. (1984). *Music, music for everyone.* New York: Greenwillow Books. (Compounds include: *something, upstairs, anything, everything, Grandma, into, without, downstairs, daytime, anyone, backyard, rosebush, everyone.*)

Chapter Book

Levinson, N.S. (1992). *Snowshoe Thompson.* New York: HarperCollins. (Compounds include: *snowshoes, wintertime, everyone, sundown, sunup, outside, mailbag, cannot.*)

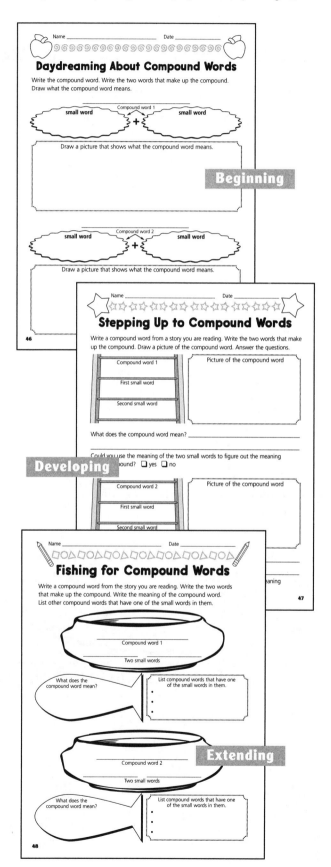

Daydreaming About Compound Words

Write the compound word. Write the two words that make up the compound.
Draw what the compound word means.

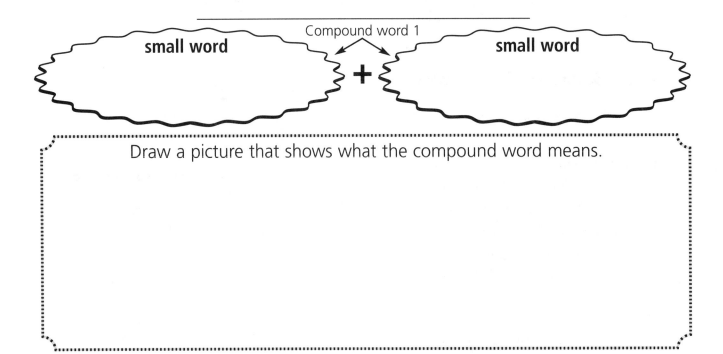

Compound word 1

small word   **+**   **small word**

Draw a picture that shows what the compound word means.

Compound word 2

small word   **+**   **small word**

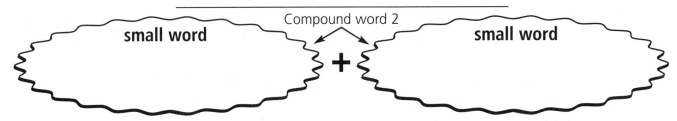

Draw a picture that shows what the compound word means.

Stepping Up to Compound Words

Write a compound word from a story you are reading. Write the two words that make up the compound. Draw a picture of the compound word. Answer the questions.

Compound word 1

First small word

Second small word

Picture of the compound word

What does the compound word mean? _____

_____

Could you use the meaning of the two small words to figure out the meaning of the compound?   ❑ yes   ❑ no

Compound word 2

First small word

Second small word

Picture of the compound word

What does the compound word mean? _____

_____

Could you use the meaning of the two small words to figure out the meaning of the compound?   ❑ yes   ❑ no

Fishing for Compound Words

Write a compound word from the story you are reading. Write the two words that make up the compound. Write the meaning of the compound word. List other compound words that have one of the small words in them.

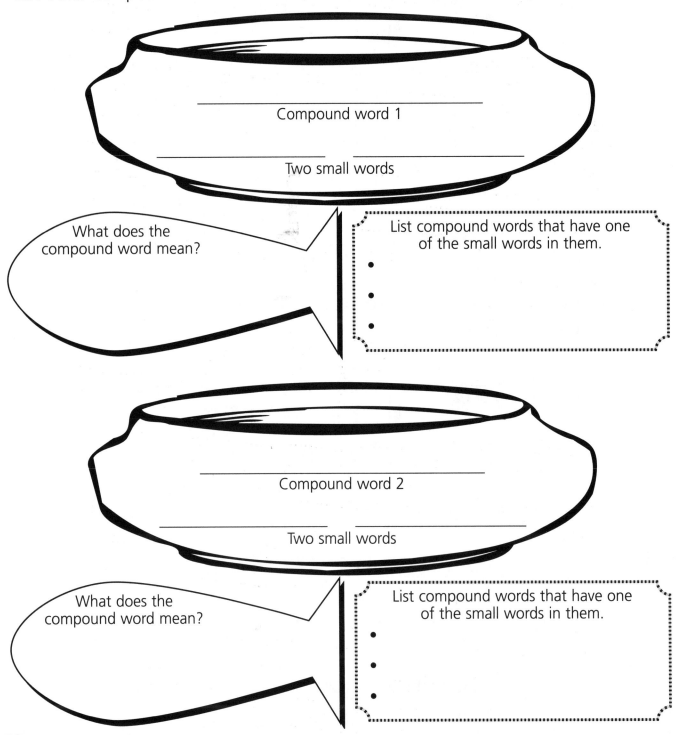

Compound word 1

_____ _____
Two small words

What does the compound word mean?

List compound words that have one of the small words in them.
-
-
-

Compound word 2

_____ _____
Two small words

What does the compound word mean?

List compound words that have one of the small words in them.
-
-
-

Synonyms

Skill: *Identify and learn words with the same meanings.*

Description

Synonyms are words that either mean the same thing or are similar in meaning, such as *rich* and *wealthy*. Besides aiding in comprehension, an awareness of synonyms allows students to communicate with more concise, descriptive language. Learning synonyms helps enlarge students' vocabulary by building a mental network of word connections. In addition, knowledge of synonyms helps students make abstract comparisons of like to like—for example, relating *big* to *large*, *huge* to *gigantic*. Using familiar words to make connections to unfamiliar words is important for word understanding and retention. Making these connections is especially essential for English language learners.

When teaching synonyms, help students consider the function and precise meaning of any substituted words. For example, if you are asking for a synonym for *big* in describing a big man, *tall* is a fine replacement. This same synonym would not work to describe a big pizza, however. It is important for students to understand that not all words have synonyms. When students are choosing a word from the text, they need to confidently choose one that fits in the given context. Apply the new word as if using a cloze procedure.

Getting to Know the Concept

Use concrete items or pictures to begin teaching the concept of synonyms. Show a familiar item and name it using a word that is less familiar to the students. Have students give synonyms for the item. For example, show a picture of a baby, but say and write the word *infant*. Ask students what word they would use, and once they answer *baby* write it on a chart beside *infant*. Pictures of the following items can be used: *lady, lavatory, bungalow, summit, cloak, pebble, doze,* and *baggage*.

Word given by teacher (with picture)	Students' response
lady	woman
lavatory	bathroom, restroom, toilet
bungalow	house, cottage, homestead
summit	mountaintop, peak
doze	nap, sleep, snooze

Teaching the Concept With Literature

Although we purposely used nouns in building the concept, other parts of speech also offer opportunities to teach synonyms. When reading to the class, select action verbs from the text that have a synonym and ask students what other words could replace the one selected. For example, if the text says, "The car sped down the hill," ask what word or words could be use to replace *sped*, such as *raced* or *rushed*. Then say the sentence filling in the synonym to see if it makes sense. Apply the new word as if using a cloze procedure.

Model Lesson

Choose a book that offers one or two short sentences per page, such as *Warthogs in the Kitchen: A Sloppy Counting Book* (Edwards, 1998). This simple format allows easy use of the cloze procedure. Read the book to the class for pleasure, then reread and ask students to give synonyms for words you select. Write the word from the text and the synonyms students give on a chart. After students suggest a synonym, use it to replace the word and read the sentence. For example, the first page of *Warthogs in the Kitchen* reads, "One little chef thinks he'll cook today." Using the word *little*, students give synonyms *small* and *tiny*. Substitute each of the synonyms in the sentence, "One *small* chef thinks he'll cook today" and "One *tiny* chef thinks he'll cook today." Ask the class if changing the word leaves the meaning about the same. If so, write the synonyms on the chart. Continue with this procedure throughout the book.

Explain how word choice can enhance a story. Have students suggest other sentences in which the synonyms can be used, such as "The boy *washed* in the bathroom" becomes "The boy *bathed* [*cleaned* or *scrubbed*] in the bathroom." Lead a discussion as to which word sounds the most interesting and have students explain why. A student might choose the word *scrubbed* because it sounds like the boy was really dirty. Explain that although words may be synonyms, sometimes the meaning changes slightly, as with *washed* and *scrubbed*.

For additional practice, have each student complete an organizer at his or her skill level.

Word from book	Synonym(s)
little	small, tiny
washed	bathed, cleaned, scrubbed
check	see, know, understand
should	must, do, ought
beat	stir, mix, whip, blend

Graphic Organizers

Beginning: **Synonym Toast** (page 52)
Students write a sentence from the book and replace one word with a synonym.

Developing: **Synonym Pairs** (page 53)
Students write a sentence from their book. They give a synonym for one word. They then rewrite the sentence substituting the synonym for the original word.

Extending: **Setting Sail with Synonyms** (page 54)
Students choose a sentence from their book and then write one word from the sentence. They list synonyms for the word. They then rewrite the sentence substituting their best synonym for the original word. They explain whether the new word makes the sentence better or not.

Great Books for This Activity

Picture Books

Dodds, D.A. (2002). *The Kettles get new clothes.* Cambridge, MA: Candlewick.

Edwards, P.D. (1998). *Warthogs in the kitchen: A sloppy counting book.* New York: Hyperion.

Lionni, L. (1991). *Matthew's dream.* New York: Knopf.

Chapter Book

Brown, J. (2003). *Stanley, flat again.* New York: HarperCollins.

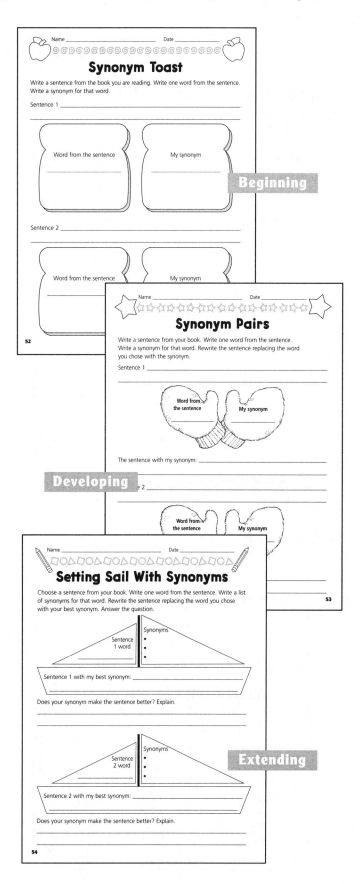

Synonym Toast

Write a sentence from the book you are reading. Write one word from the sentence. Write a synonym for that word.

Sentence 1 _____

_____

Word from the sentence

_____

My synonym

_____

Sentence 2 _____

_____

Word from the sentence

_____

My synonym

_____

Synonym Pairs

Write a sentence from your book. Write one word from the sentence.
Write a synonym for that word. Rewrite the sentence replacing the word
you chose with the synonym.

Sentence 1 _____

_____

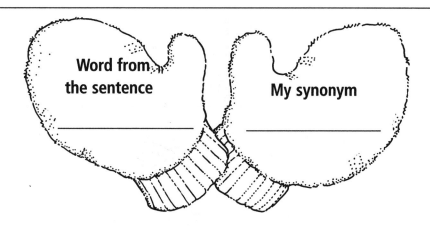

**Word from
the sentence**

_____

My synonym

_____

The sentence with my synonym: _____

_____

Sentence 2 _____

_____

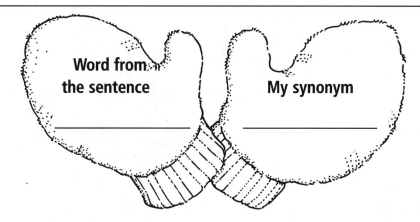

**Word from
the sentence**

_____

My synonym

_____

The sentence with my synonym: _____

_____

Setting Sail With Synonyms

Choose a sentence from your book. Write one word from the sentence. Write a list of synonyms for that word. Rewrite the sentence replacing the word you chose with your best synonym. Answer the question.

Sentence 1 word

_____

Synonyms
-
-
-

Sentence 1 with my best synonym: _____

_____

Does your synonym make the sentence better? Explain.

_____

_____

Sentence 2 word

_____

Synonyms
-
-
-

Sentence 2 with my best synonym: _____

_____

Does your synonym make the sentence better? Explain.

_____

_____

Antonyms

Skill: *Recognize words with opposite meanings.*

Description

Contrasts have been used for centuries to amplify important concepts, to gain attention, and to make statements much more colorful and interesting. Note the antonyms in the famous quotes, "It was the best of times, it was the worst of times. . . ." (Dickens) and "for better for worse, for richer for poorer, in sickness and in health. . . ." (Book of Common Prayer). Antonyms are words with opposite meanings. Antonyms can be two completely different words like *short* and *tall* or they can be differentiated by a prefix like *common* and *uncommon*.

Knowledge of antonyms can strengthen students' vocabulary in a variety of ways. Good readers use their understanding of the antonym relationship to help figure out a word's meaning in context. Recognizing antonyms aids in comprehension. An understanding of antonyms can help students contrast people, places, things, and ideas.

Getting to Know the Concept

Although *antonyms* is the correct terminology, most students understand the term *opposites*. Begin by explaining that an antonym is the same as an opposite. To help students grasp the concept, play an action game.

Pair students for "Antonym Partners." Explain that each person in the partnership will "play" one of the antonyms. Label each partner A or B. Tell partner A to show a sad face and partner B to show a happy face. Explain that *happy* and *sad* are antonyms. Now have partner A and B switch roles in which partner A shows a happy face, and partner B shows a sad face. Follow this procedure with the following antonym commands. Remind students that each pair of words are antonyms because they mean the opposite.

Antonym	Partner A (then B)	Partner B (then A)
high/low	point high	point low
cold/hot	shiver	wipe your brow
fast/slow	talk fast	talk slowly
close/open	close your mouth	open your mouth
up/down	look up	look down
awake/asleep	be wide awake	pretend to sleep

Teaching the Concept With Literature

Beginning picture books that feature opposites are published in abundance and are ideal for teaching the concept: the pictures are big and the antonyms are simple. A quick online search for "picture books: opposites" yields plenty of examples, from Tana Hoban's *Exactly the Opposite* (1993) to Remy Charlip's classic *Fortunately* (1964). You might use these books to reteach the concept, and then continue to follow up, pointing out antonyms in your read-alouds and asking students to show examples from their independent reading. For example, after reading *Strega Nona* (de Paola, 1975) revisit the first page with the class. As you read, stop at words that have opposites and share with the students. The following antonyms can be found at the beginning of *Strega Nona: long/short, lived/died, old/young, lady/gentleman, everyone/no one, all/none, town/country, whispers/shouts, sisters/brothers.*

Model Lesson

This lesson's goal is to emphasize that some words have antonyms and to aid students in identifying words that have one or more antonyms. Begin the lesson by reviewing antonyms. Explain that authors choose words carefully, and that an author deliberately makes a character little instead of big, large instead of small, happy instead of sad, and nice instead of mean. Authors may make characters change into the opposite as part of the story line—sometimes a mean character becomes nice, a sloppy character becomes neat, or a poor character becomes rich.

Choose a language-rich book, such as *Mrs. McTats and Her Houseful of Cats* (Capucilli, 2001). Read it first for enjoyment, and then reread to teach and reinforce antonyms. Write the title on the board and ask students if they recognize words with antonyms, such as *Mrs.* and *Mr.* and *full* and *empty.* Ask students to locate words that are antonyms, and to name as many antonyms that they can for the word. Write them on the chart. Working in partners, have students say a sentence using the antonyms. Write the sentence on the chart.

For additional practice, have each student complete an organizer at his or her skill level.

Graphic Organizers

Beginning: **Antonym Artist** (page 58)
Students select two words that have antonyms from the chart or from a book. They draw a picture representing each word and its antonym.

Word from book	Antonyms	Sentence
small	large, big, gigantic, huge	My dog is small, but her dog is big.
cozy	uncomfortable, unpleasant	Would you say the house was cozy or uncomfortable?
cottage	mansion, castle, palace	The little cottage is beside the tall mansion.
every	none, zero	I have every transformer but my cousin has none.

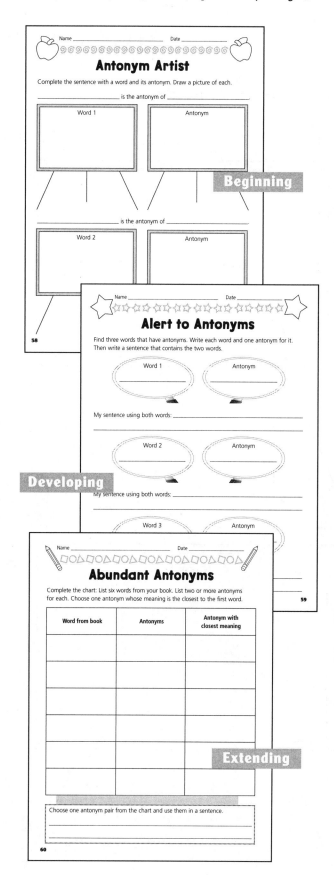

Developing: **Alert to Antonyms** (page 59)
From the chart or from a book students select three words that have antonyms. They write each word and its antonym and then create a sentence that contains the two words.

Extending: **Abundant Antonyms** (page 60)
Students select six words from the chart or from a book. Each should have more than one antonym. They identify one that has the closest meaning to the original word. They choose one pair of antonyms to use in a sentence that illustrates the word meanings.

Great Books for This Activity

Picture Books

Capucilli, A.S. (2001). *Mrs. McTats and her houseful of cats.* New York: McElderry.

Charlip, R. (1964). *Fortunately.* New York: Parents Magazine Press.

de Paola, T. (1975). *Strega Nona: An old tale.* Englewood Cliffs, NJ: Prentice-Hall.

Ganeri, A. (2001). *The story of Columbus.* New York: Dorling Kindersley.

Hoban, T. (1997). *Exactly the opposite.* New York: Harper.

Zion, G. (1956). *Harry the dirty dog.* New York: Harper.

Chapter Book

Adler, D.A. (1980). *Jan Camsen, the mystery of the stolen diamonds.* New York: Viking.

Antonym Artist

Complete the sentence with a word and its antonym. Draw a picture of each.

_____ is the antonym of _____ .

Word 1	Antonym

_____ is the antonym of _____ .

Word 2	Antonym

Alert to Antonyms

Find three words that have antonyms. Write each word and one antonym for it. Then write a sentence that contains the two words.

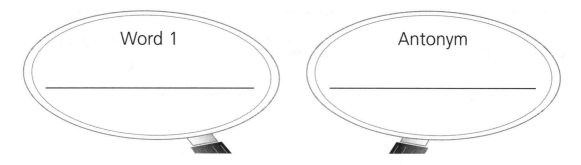

Word 1

Antonym

My sentence using both words: _____

_____

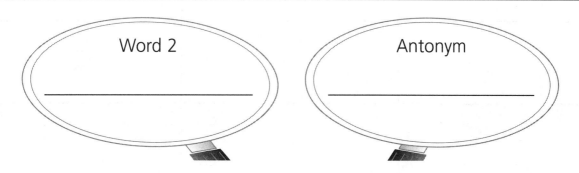

Word 2

Antonym

My sentence using both words: _____

_____

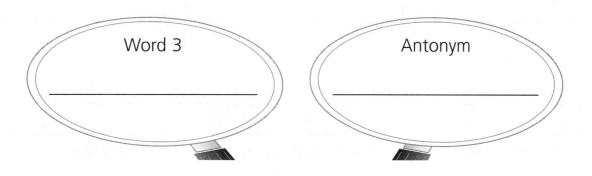

Word 3

Antonym

My sentence using both words: _____

_____

Abundant Antonyms

Complete the chart: List six words from your book. List two or more antonyms for each. Choose one antonym whose meaning is the closest to the first word.

Word from book	Antonyms	Antonym with closest meaning

Choose one antonym pair from the chart and use them in a sentence.

_____

_____

Homophones

Skill: *Recognize that words can sound the same but have different spellings and meanings.*

Description

When students realize that some words sound the same but are spelled differently and carry with them different meanings, they often become passionate about hunting for examples of these "twin" words, such as *sea* and *see*; *by, bye,* and *buy*; or *sun* and *son*. A disposition to learn about words is called word consciousness. Word-conscious students are able to think metacognitively about words, are motivated to learn new words, and take an interest in words. Helping all students develop word consciousness can have a lasting impact on their reading comprehension, writing proficiency, and word usage for English language learners (Graves, 2006). When working with homophones, focus on word-conscious behaviors, including considering why writers use particular words in various contexts.

Getting to Know the Concept

Write the word *which* on a piece of card stock. Read the word aloud and show a picture of a *witch*. Acknowledge that the two words sound alike. Write the word *witch* under the picture and discuss the differences in how the words are spelled. Repeat the procedure with the word *toe* and a picture of a *tow* truck. Introduce and define the word *homophone*.

To prepare for a concentration-type game, write each of the following words on separate index cards: *night* and *knight*; *sail* and *sale*; *hair* and *hare*; *plain* and *plane*; and *hi* and *high*. Discuss the words and their definitions. Divide students into groups of four and have them place the cards face down on a table. Have a student in each group turn over two cards to see if they are homophone pairs. If found, the student keeps the pair. If not, the cards are returned face down to their original spot and another student selects two cards, looking for a homophone pair.

Review the term *homophones* and build interest by having students look for additional examples. You might conclude this lesson by pointing out that finding homophones is not only fun, but also a way for students to learn new, interesting words.

Teaching the Concept With Literature

Choose a well-loved picture book, such as *Miss Rumphius* (Cooney, 1982), to introduce the concept of homophones. Students may be familiar with the world-traveling Miss Rumphius, but they may be less familiar with the specific words the author uses. After reading the book, write the following words on chart paper: *sea, blue, know, so, by, wood, ate, there, sun,* and *flower*. Help students pair each word with a homophone. Discuss the definition of each word. Suggest that students be on the lookout for homophones they see and hear throughout the day. Add these words to the list. Focusing on homophones will help students build word consciousness and extend their oral and written vocabularies.

Model Lesson

Choose a book with homophones, such as *Walter the Baker* (Carle, 1995). This humorous book tells how Walter succeeds in creating the world's first pretzel. Create a four-column chart. Write the following homophones from the book in the first column: *son, whole, one, flower, threw, piece, night, vain, there, pail, sent, pray,* and *dough*.

After reading the book for pleasure, display the chart. Together with students, complete the second column. Then write homophones in the third column and together complete the fourth column.

Demonstrate how you can create a meaningful sentence using a pair of homophones, for example, *The person who **won** the raffle was the lucky **one***. After sharing a few examples, ask students to work with a partner or triad to create their own sentences. Then have students share their sentences with the class. Review the definition of homophones and remind students that they should keep an eye out for homophones while reading and listening.

For additional practice, have each student complete an organizer at his or her skill level.

Graphic Organizers

Beginning: **Hearing Double** (page 64)
Students draw and label teacher-determined pairs of homophones.

Word	I could use this word when	Word	I could use this word when
son	I'm talking about a father and his little boy	sun	I'm thinking about the solar system
whole	I'm describing something that is complete	hole	I'm writing about what my puppy dug in the backyard
one	I have more than zero and less than two	won	I'm describing a basketball game where the score was 56 to 48
flower	I'm talking about tulips and roses	flour	I'm talking about a person baking bread

Developing: **Twin Words** (page 65)
Students list three teacher-determined pairs of homophones and explain when each word can be used.

Extending: **Hear Here!** (page 66)
Students list two teacher-determined pairs of homophones and explain when each word can be used. For each set of homophones, students also write a sentence that contains the pair of homophones. Finally, they list their own pair of homophones and write a sentence using both words.

Great Books for This Activity

Picture Books

Carle, E. (1995). *Walter the baker*. New York: Simon & Schuster.

Cooney, B (1982). *Miss Rumphius*.
New York: Puffin.

DePaola, T. (1984). *The mysterious giant of Barletta: An Italian folktale*. San Diego: Harcourt. (Homophones include: *one, knew, there, right, sun, sell, by, to, night, peace, here, do, high.*)

DePaola, T. (2005). *Stagestruck*. New York: Putnam's Sons. (Homophones include: *spring, play, lines, tap, knew, too, stand, night, way.*)

Chapter Book

Greene, S. (2006). *Pig pickin'*. Tarrytown, NY: Marshall Cavendish. (Homophones include: *piece, where, too, right, fair, I, one.*)

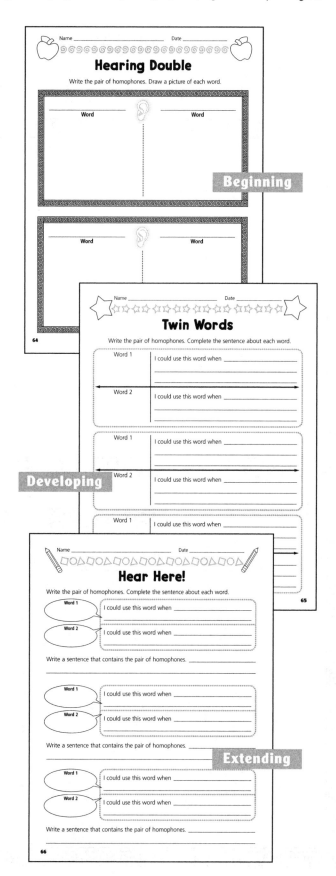

Hearing Double

Write the pair of homophones. Draw a picture of each word.

_____ **Word**   **Word** _____

_____ **Word**   **Word** _____

Twin Words

Write the pair of homophones. Complete the sentence about each word.

Word 1

I could use this word when _____

_____

_____

Word 2

I could use this word when _____

_____

_____

Word 1

I could use this word when _____

_____

_____

Word 2

I could use this word when _____

_____

_____

Word 1

I could use this word when _____

_____

_____

Word 2

I could use this word when _____

_____

_____

Hear Here!

Write the pair of homophones. Complete the sentence about each word.

Word 1

I could use this word when _____

_____

Word 2

I could use this word when _____

_____

Write a sentence that contains the pair of homophones. _____

_____

Word 1

I could use this word when _____

_____

Word 2

I could use this word when _____

_____

Write a sentence that contains the pair of homophones. _____

_____

Word 1

I could use this word when _____

_____

Word 2

I could use this word when _____

_____

Write a sentence that contains the pair of homophones. _____

_____

Idioms

Skill: *To recognize that idioms have a figurative, rather than literal, meaning.*

Description

An idiom is an expression that cannot be understood from a literal reading. For instance, the phrases *go fly a kite* and *go jump in a lake* both mean "leave" or "get out of here." The meaning has nothing to do with either a kite or a lake.

Idioms are especially difficult for English language learners, who often take each word at face value as they process spoken and written English. While native-born students might grow up hearing that they need to "step on it" to hurry them along, English language learners process the phrase literally. They might translate it as having something to do with stairs, and then begin to wonder where everyone is going and what will be stepped on. Be sure to give these students the extra support and practice they need to recognize common idioms. English-proficient students can begin to use idioms to add humor and voice in their writing.

Getting to Know the Concept

Ask students what you mean when you say a familiar idiom, such as *step on it* or *keep your fingers crossed*. Ask what this expression would look like if they were to draw a picture. Does what it looks like have any connection to what it means? Explain that idioms have their own meaning, just like words. Throughout the school day, state common idioms when appropriate and ask students to tell you what the idiom means. Some examples include:

butterflies in your tummy   *it's as easy as pie*

on the right track   *quit horsing around*

knock it off   *don't spill the beans*

don't make a pig of yourself   *has the cat got your tongue?*

piece of cake

Teaching the Concept With Literature

Once students understand the concept of idioms, help them identify and understand idioms in their everyday reading. As you read aloud, make a point of commenting on idioms and ask students if they can get an idea from the text. For example, in *Lovable Lyle* (Waber, 1969), we find "Lyle *lost himself* in play." In *Pigsty* (Teague, 1994) the title itself represents an idiom (*like a pigsty*), and the book illustrates the literal view of a pigsty. Discuss what is happening in the text when you encounter idioms, and help students interpret their meaning.

Model Lesson

Choose a book with several idioms. The queen of misinterpreting idioms is Amelia Bedelia (Parish), and any Amelia Bedelia book will work well with this lesson. As you read *Amelia Bedelia 4 Mayor* (Parish, 1999), stop and discuss each idiom to make sure students understand what it means and compare the meaning to what Amelia, who interprets everything literally, thinks it means. For example, Amelia is told she should "run for the mayor's office" and she immediately

takes off running to the mayor's office. She misinterprets the "the mayor has very big shoes to fill" as an insult about the size of the mayor's feet. As you read this book, chart the idioms, and their correct meanings, as shown below.

Review the completed chart with students. Ask them to visualize and explain what Amelia is thinking as she takes each idiom literally. Have students use each idiomatic expression in a sentence of their own.

For additional practice, have each student complete an organizer at his or her skill level.

Graphic Organizers

Beginning: **As Easy As Pie** (page 70)
Students write two idioms from their books, draw the literal definitions, and write what the expressions really mean under the picture.

Developing: **Picture Perfect** (page 71)
Students copy two idioms from their books

Idiom	What it really means	Amelia thinks and sees...
big shoes to fill	has done a fantastic job	his feet are big
my two cents	my opinion	two pennies
throw your hat in the ring	agree to run for office or do what people are doing	throws a hat on a telephone
sitting on the fence	people haven't made up their minds	people are sitting on a fence with sore bottoms
cut the red tape	get rid of paperwork and rules that aren't necessary	takes scissors and cut a red ribbon
fighting like cats and dogs	very angry, yelling	a cat and dog are fighting

and copy the sentence in which each idiom appears. Then they draw the literal meaning of the idiom and the actual meaning. Finally, they write the actual meaning of the idiom.

Extending: **Step On It!** (page 72)
Students copy two idioms from their books and copy the sentence in which each idiom appears. They then define the idiom and write a new sentence using it. Students choose one idiom and draw the literal meaning.

Great Books for This Activity

Picture Books
Parish, H. (1999). *Amelia Bedelia 4 mayor.* New York: Greenwillow.

Parish, P. (1976). *Good work, Amelia Bedelia.* New York: Greenwillow.

Teague, M. (1994). *Pigsty.* New York: Scholastic.

Waber, B. (1969). *Lovable Lyle.* Boston, MA: Houghton Mifflin.

Chapter Book
Dahl, R. (1981). *George's marvelous medicine.* New York: Knopf. (Idioms include: *bored to tears, hair standing straight up,* and *eyes popped out.*)

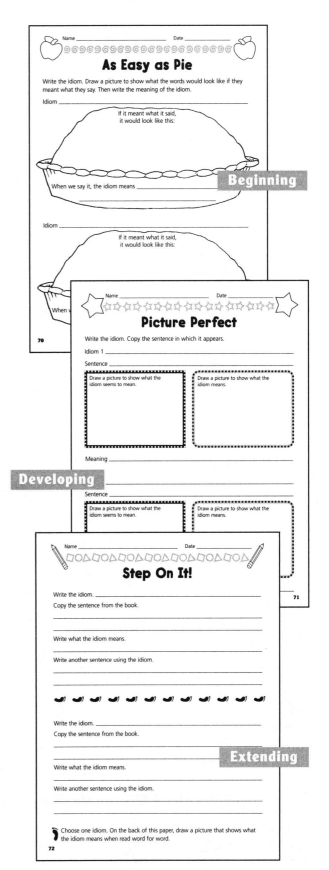

As Easy as Pie

Write the idiom. Draw a picture to show what the words would look like if they meant what they say. Then write the meaning of the idiom.

Idiom _____

If it meant what it said,
it would look like this:

When we say it, the idiom means _____

_____

Idiom _____

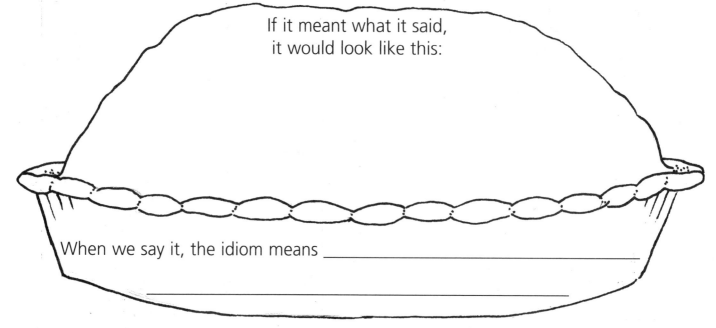

If it meant what it said,
it would look like this:

When we say it, the idiom means _____

_____

Picture Perfect

Write the idiom. Copy the sentence in which it appears.

Idiom 1 _____

Sentence _____

Draw a picture to show what the idiom seems to mean.

Draw a picture to show what the idiom means.

Meaning _____

Idiom 2 _____

Sentence _____

Draw a picture to show what the idiom seems to mean.

Draw a picture to show what the idiom means.

Meaning _____

Step On It!

Write the idiom. _____

Copy the sentence from the book.

_____

_____

Write what the idiom means.

_____

Write another sentence using the idiom.

_____

_____

Write the idiom. _____

Copy the sentence from the book.

_____

_____

Write what the idiom means.

_____

Write another sentence using the idiom.

_____

_____

 Choose one idiom. On the back of this paper, draw a picture that shows what
the idiom means when read word for word.

Prefixes <u>un</u> and <u>re</u>

Skill: *Recognize that prefixes are groups of letters that are added to the beginning of a base word to create a new word.*

Description

An awareness of prefixes enables students to build on meanings they already know in order to figure out the meanings of new words. According to an analysis conducted by White, Sowell, and Yanigihara (1989), the following prefixes account for 76% of all prefixed words: *un, re, in, im, ir, il, dis, en* and *em, non, in* and *im, over,* and *mis*. These few prefixes have a profound impact on word meaning. If students know, for example, that *un* can mean *not* or *the opposite of*, they understand that *unsafe* means *not safe*. If they know that *re* means *to do something again* or *repeatedly*, they recognize that *rewind* means *to wind something again*. In this chapter we focus on *un* and *re*, but the activities can be applied to all prefixes.

Getting to Know the Concept

Introduce the concept of prefixes by holding up a card on which you've written *un*. Explain that *un* can mean *not* or *the opposite of*. Say the word *happy* and then hold up the *un* card and say *unhappy*. Discuss how the meaning of *happy* changes when joined with *un*. Continue to introduce the following base words and new words: *wind* and *unwind, even* and *uneven, friendly* and *unfriendly,* and *pack* and *unpack*. Discuss how adding *un* changes the meaning of the base words. Have students complete the following sentences that contain a word with the prefix *un*:

I can go into the room without a key because the door is (unlocked).

Jill might trip and fall because her shoelace is (untied).

Even though Ben found a magic coin, he still feels (unlucky).

Hold up a card on which you've written *re*. Explain that *re* is a prefix that means *to do again* or *repeatedly*. Have individual students dramatize the following sentences:

Enter and then reenter the room.

Fill and then refill the pitcher of water.

Write and then rewrite the word *cat*.

After each sentence, pause to talk about the action and how the prefix *re* influenced what each student did. Summarize by pointing out that knowing what a prefix means can help students figure out the meaning of unfamiliar words.

Teaching the Concept With Literature

It may be difficult to find many books that have multiple examples of the prefixes *un* and *re* in them, particularly if your students are reading easy readers. When you do come across examples, point out the base word, the prefix, the new word, and the word's meaning. In *"Let's Get a Pup!" Said Kate* (Graham, 2001) is the word *uneaten*. In *Annie and the Wild Animals* (Brett, 1985) is the word *unexpected*. You may need to excerpt selections from more advanced books or basal readers that have passages that feature prefixes.

Model Lesson

Before introducing prefixes, teach students how to identify base words (words that can stand alone) such as *wrap* or *play*. Explain that prefixes are added to base words to create new, related words, such as *unwrap* or *replay*. List the following words on a chart: *rebuild, reseed, unlike, uneven, unable*.

Taking one word at a time, draw a box around each base word and write the base word in the center column. Confirm that each base word is a real word. Write the following words on the board: *uncle, under, reach, recess*. Place a box around each *un* or *re* and explain that since the base word in each is not a word, *un* and *re* are not prefixes in these

words. Remind students that not all words beginning with *un* or *re* are words with a prefix and base word. Explain that when words do have a prefix, we can use the prefix to help unlock the meaning of word.

Return to the *un* words on the chart and ask students if they can figure out what *un* means in these words (*not* or *the opposite of*). Confirm by having them use each word in a sentence. Have students brainstorm other words that begin with *un*, write them on the chart, divide the prefix and base word to ensure that the word has a prefix, and use the prefix to define the new word. Once students are familiar with *un*, repeat this process with the *re* words on your chart.

Have students brainstorm what they think of when they hear each new word on the chart (what associations can they make). For example, students might associate *replay* with a video or DVD or an instant replay in a TV football game. Record responses in the last column on the chart.

For additional practice, have each student complete an organizer at his or her skill level.

Graphic Organizers

Beginning: **Uncovering New Words** (page 76)
Using two words the teacher provides, students divide each word into a prefix

New word	Base word	Association
re play	play	video, DVD, instant replay

and a base word. They write the word's meaning and then draw a picture showing the meaning of the new word.

Developing: **Recalling Familiar Words**
(page 77)
Using two words the teacher provides, students divide each word into a prefix and a base word. They write the meaning of the base word and of the new word. Students also demonstrate their understanding of each new word by making associations between the word and their experiences.

Extending: **Replacing Word Meanings**
(page 78)
Using two words the teacher provides, students define each new word, make associations between the words and their experiences, and use each new word in a sentence.

Great Books for This Activity

Picture Books

Brett, J. (1985). *Annie and the wild animals.* Boston, MA: Houghton Mifflin.

Graham, B. (2001). *"Let's get a pup!" said Kate.* Cambridge, MA: Candlewick.

Wong, J.S. (2000). *The trip back home.* San Diego: Harcourt.

Chapter Book

Lowry, L. (2002). *Gooney Bird Greene.* Boston, MA: Houghton Mifflin. (Words with prefixes include: *unusual, unscrewed, unfortunately, unanswered, unbuttoned, returned, research;* non-examples include: *under, required, until, replied, rescue, reward, remember.*)

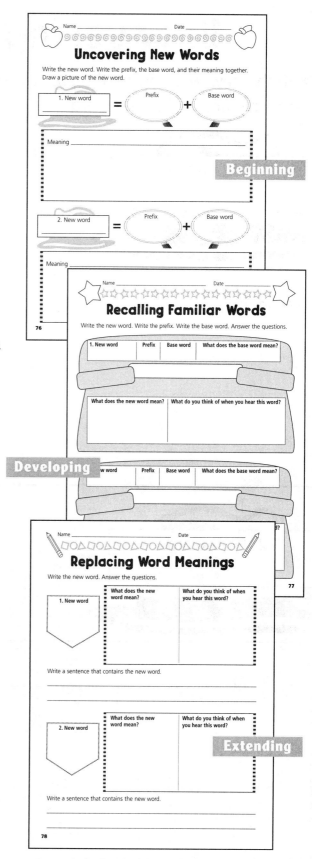

Uncovering New Words

Write the new word. Write the prefix, the base word, and their meaning together.
Draw a picture of the new word.

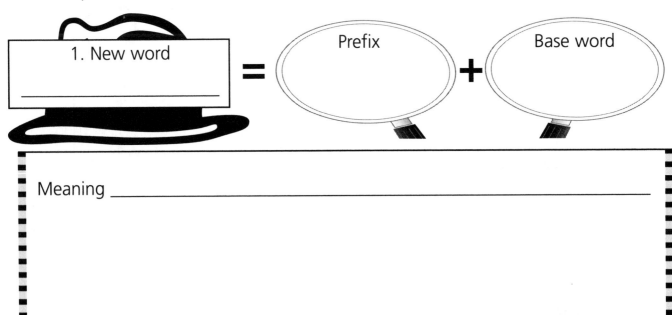

1. New word _____ = Prefix ( ) + Base word ( )

Meaning _____

2. New word _____ = Prefix ( ) + Base word ( )

Meaning _____

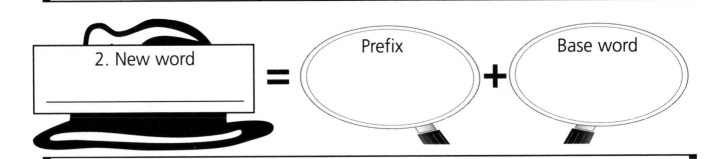

Recalling Familiar Words

Write the new word. Write the prefix. Write the base word. Answer the questions.

1. New word	Prefix	Base word	What does the base word mean?

What does the new word mean?	What do you think of when you hear this word?

2. New word	Prefix	Base word	What does the base word mean?

What does the new word mean?	What do you think of when you hear this word?

Replacing Word Meanings

Write the new word. Answer the questions.

1. New word	What does the new word mean?	What do you think of when you hear this word?

Write a sentence that contains the new word.

_____

_____

2. New word	What does the new word mean?	What do you think of when you hear this word?

Write a sentence that contains the new word.

_____

_____

Suffixes -er and -or

Skill: *Recognize that suffixes are groups of letters that are added to the end of a base word to create a new word.*
Note: We recommend teaching suffixes after teaching the Prefixes chapter (page 73).

Description

When *-er* or *-or* is added to a base word, the verb changes into a noun that names what someone does, such as an occupation or hobby. For example, someone who skates (v) is a *skater* (n); someone who invents (v) is an *inventor* (n). Understanding suffixes helps students enhance their oral and written vocabularies. It makes evident the relationships between words.

Getting to Know the Concept

Explain to students that we name a person who does a job or hobby by adding *-er* or *-or* to what they do. For example, a person who farms is a *farmer*. Point out illustrations and photos on book covers that show people doing jobs or hobbies whose names end in *-er* or *-or*, such as *firefighter, explorer, dancer, sailor, hiker, gardener*. For example, you might hold up the cover of *Not Afraid of Dogs* (Pitzer, 2006) and say, "This woman is walking dogs. She is a *dog walker*." Continue with other book covers and discuss base words and words with *-er* or *-or* suffixes that name jobs and hobbies.

Teaching the Concept With Literature

As you and your students read texts, be on the lookout for base words to which *-er* or *-or* have been added. Take advantage of opportunities to delve into word histories and to discuss connections between base words and related words. For example, for the word *plumber*, explain that *plumb* is a small mound of lead or heavy metal. The relationship between the base word *plumb* and new word *plumber* is not as well known as some other words. Once students know this, they should be able to understand how the words *plumb* and *plumber* are related.

Model Lesson

Choose a book with with *-er* and *-or* words, such as *My Teacher's Secret Life* (Krensky, 1996). In this humorous book, the narrator's assumptions about his teacher are challenged when he sees her out in the community. After reading the book, return to the cover and point to the word *teacher*. Point out that a teacher is someone who teaches. Prepare a three-column chart and record *teaches/teacher*. Pause when Mrs. Quirk is filling her cart at the supermarket. Point out that Mrs. Quirk is someone who is shopping, so she is a *shopper*. Add the words to the chart and continue with the story. Pause on the page that shows Mrs. Quirk in roller skates. Explain that Mrs. Quirk is someone who skates so she is a *skater*. Record the words on the chart.

In order to deepen students' understanding of word meanings, use the think aloud process to identify the types of objects each person would likely use for the job or hobby. Record these on the chart.

Use each word that contains a suffix *-er* or *-or* in an original sentence that demonstrates an understanding of each word's meaning. Remind students that words with suffixes *-er* or *-or* sometimes indicate a job or hobby.

For additional practice, have each student complete an organizer at his or her skill level.

Graphic Organizers

Beginning: **Investigator** (page 82)
Students use two teacher-selected words with the suffixes *-er* or *-or* to complete a sentence. They draw a picture to accompany each sentence.

Developing: **Recycler** (page 83)
Students use two teacher-selected words with the suffixes *-er* or *-or* to complete a sentence. Students list objects each person would use in his or her job or hobby and write a sentence for each new word.

Extending: **Announcer** (page 84)
Students locate three words that contain *-er* or *-or* suffixes. They use the words to complete sentences. For each word, students list the objects that person would use in his or her job or hobby. They also record where they found the word and use it in a sentence.

Someone who	is a	This person might use
teaches	teacher	overhead projector, stickers, reading glasses
shops	shopper	shopping cart, brown bags, coupons, money
skates	skater	gloves, helmet, kneepads

Great Books for This Activity

Picture Books

Graham, B. (2007). *"The trouble with dogs," said Dad.* Cambridge, MA: Candlewick. (Includes *barkers, biters, breakers, post sniffers, leaping leash-tanglers, owners.*)

Kraus, R. (1971). *Leo the late bloomer.* New York: Windmill. (Includes *bloomer* and *eater.* Talk about how Leo becomes a *reader,* a *writer,* and a *speaker.*)

Krensky, S. (1996). *My teacher's secret life.* New York: Simon & Schuster.

Pitzer, S. (2006). *Not afraid of dogs.* New York: Walker.

Chapter Book

Kline, S. (2006). *Herbie Jones sails into second grade.* New York: Putnam. (Includes *second-grader, teacher, sailor, braggers, writers, readers, operator.*)

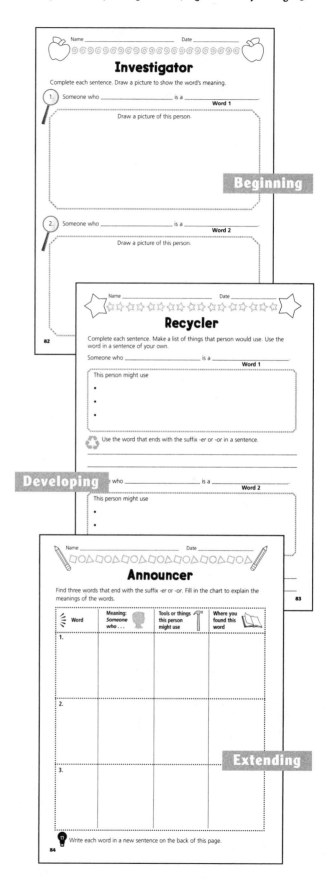

Investigator

Complete each sentence. Draw a picture to show the word's meaning.

1. Someone who _____ is a _____.

Word 1

Draw a picture of this person.

2. Someone who _____ is a _____.

Word 2

Draw a picture of this person.

Recycler

Complete each sentence. Make a list of things that person would use. Use the word in a sentence of your own.

Someone who _____ is a _____.

Word 1

This person might use

-
-
-

Use the word that ends with the suffix *-er* or *-or* in a sentence.

_____

_____

Someone who _____ is a _____.

Word 2

This person might use

-
-
-

Use the word that ends with the suffix *-er* or *-or* in a sentence.

_____

_____

Announcer

Find three words that end with the suffix -er or -or. Fill in the chart to explain the meanings of the words.

Word	Meaning: Someone who . . .	Tools or things this person might use	Where you found this word
1.			
2.			
3.			

Write each word in a new sentence on the back of this page.

Context Clues

Skill: *Reinforce the meaning of new words from pictures and texts.*

Description

An important strategy for helping readers determine the meaning or gist of an unknown word they encounter in their reading is knowing how to use context clues. This skill helps students read independently. In order to make a new word part of their vocabulary, students need practice using the word after they have inferred its meaning. Using context clues must move beyond helping students simply understand the meaning of unfamiliar words to reinforcing and retaining those meanings.

Getting to Know the Concept

Teaching students to use context clues while reading encourages them to pay attention to pictures and words that are near an unfamiliar word. In so doing, they can often find the support they need to understand the meaning of the word and its function in the surrounding text. Once students have inferred the word's meaning, take time to reinforce the word so it becomes part of the student's vocabulary. Find everyday experiences you can use to introduce and develop Tier 2 words (page 5). For example, when walking past a classroom in which children are quietly working, say, "Let's walk softly so we don't disturb this class." Stop to ask students what they think the word *disturb* means. Guide them to identify clues that helped them determine the word's meaning ("walking softly," "children working quietly"). Ask what other words mean the same as *disturb*. Reinforce the word by asking partners to tell each other about things that *disturb* them when they are trying to work. Have students share their ideas with the whole group, using the word *disturb* in their sentences. Encourage use of the new word during the day to extend its meaning beyond its original context.

Teaching the Concept With Literature

Choose a book with Tier 2 words, such as *Happy Birthday, Jamela* (Daly, 2006). Reread the section of the book in which Jamela shows her mother and grandmother how she transformed her plain black school shoes into princess shoes by gluing beads all over them. Her grandmother wanted to laugh "but wasting money was no laughing matter, so she frowned instead." Have students infer the meaning of *frowned*. Discuss how they determined the word's meaning (pictures and text). Point out how they can use pictures and words found before and after an unfamiliar word to determine its meaning.

Model Lesson

Choose a book with Tier 2 words, such as *Terrible Storm* (Hurst, 2007). You might begin with the word *shy* and write the word in its original context on chart paper. Model how you infer the meaning of this word (using the text and illustrations from the previous page as well as the illustration from this page). Write the definition on chart paper. Brainstorm with students other times or places when you might use this word. For example, *I feel <u>shy</u> when I walk into a party where I don't know anyone.* Go back to *Terrible Storm* and ask if Grandpa Clark acted shy in other situations. Ask students to generate other words or phrases they could use that mean the same or almost the same as *shy*. Write their answers on the chart paper. Review the notes you recorded on chart paper to reinforce the meaning of the word *shy*.

Remind students that when they come to an unfamiliar word in their reading, they should use context clues to figure out the word's meaning. Encourage them to connect the word to other situations and other words they know with similar meanings.

For additional practice, have each student complete an organizer at his or her skill level.

Graphic Organizers

Beginning: **Holding on to New Words** (page 88)
Provide two teacher-designated target words in a context that will help students determine their meanings. Have students infer the meaning of each word and draw a picture to reinforce the meaning. Have them label each picture with the new word.

Developing: **Locking Up Word Meanings** (page 89)
Provide two teacher-designated target words in a context that will help students determine their meanings. Students write the two new words and the sentences that contain the words. They also define the words and brainstorm other situations in which they could use each word.

Extending: **Context Clues Clipboard** (page 90)
Provide two teacher-designated target words in a context that will help students determine their meanings. Students write the two new words and the sentences that contain the words. Then they define the words and brainstorm other situations in which they could use each word. Students

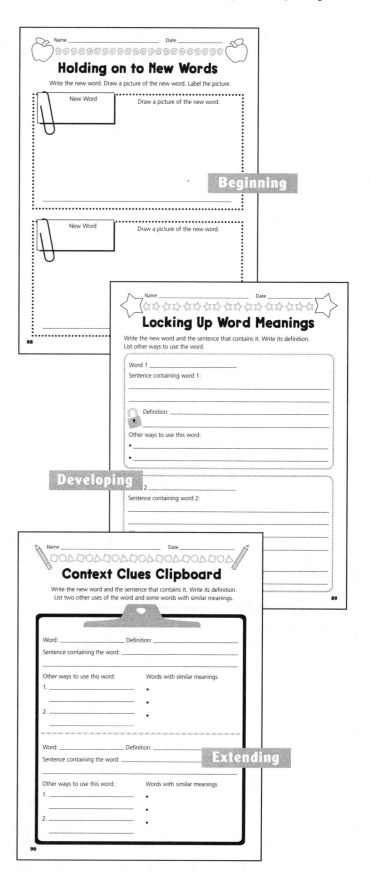

also list words or phrases that have a similar meaning.

Great Books for This Activity

Picture Books

Daly, N. (2006). *Happy birthday, Jamela!* New York: Farrar, Straus and Giroux.

Hurst, C.O. (2007). *Terrible storm*. New York: Greenwillow.

Juster, N. (2005). *The hello, goodbye window*. New York: Hyperion Books. (Tier 2 words include: *reflections, specialty, expect, extinct.*)

Park, F. and Park, G. (2002). *Good-bye, 382 Shin Dang Dong*. Washington, DC: National Geographic. (Tier 2 words include: *possessions, peered, moaned, attached.*)

Chapter Book

Rylant, C. (2005). *The case of the desperate duck (High-Rise Private Eyes)*. New York: Greenwillow. (Tier 2 words include: *heights, counter, disappoint.*)

Holding on to New Words

Write the new word. Draw a picture of the new word. Label the picture.

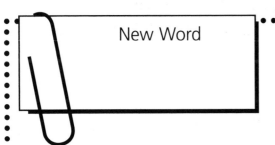

New Word

Draw a picture of the new word.

_____

New Word

Draw a picture of the new word.

_____

Locking Up Word Meanings

Write the new word and the sentence that contains it. Write its definition.
List other ways to use the word.

Word 1 _____

Sentence containing word 1:

_____

_____

Definition: _____

_____

Other ways to use this word:

- _____

- _____

Word 2 _____

Sentence containing word 2:

_____

_____

Definition: _____

_____

Other ways to use this word:

- _____

- _____

Context Clues Clipboard

Write the new word and the sentence that contains it. Write its definition.
List two other uses of the word and some words with similar meanings.

Word: _____ Definition: _____

Sentence containing the word: _____

_____

Other ways to use this word: Words with similar meanings

1. _____   •

    _____   •

2. _____   •

    _____

Word: _____ Definition: _____

Sentence containing the word: _____

_____

Other ways to use this word: Words with similar meanings

1. _____   •

    _____   •

2. _____   •

    _____

Replacing Overused Words

Skill: *Select overused words and replace them with more interesting or specific ones.*

Note: We recommend working with the activities in this chapter after teaching the Synonyms chapter (page 49).

Description

A large number of primary-level books are written with simplified language. Many of these books are decodable and written to ensure students read on their instructional level. Unfortunately, reading these books does not encourage students' vocabulary acquisition. Additional instruction is needed to help students acquire a wealth of stronger and more accurate vocabulary so they can communicate clearly and more precisely. For example, a child may say, "The candy tasted yucky," when, in fact, it tasted bitter, sour, tart, sweet, syrupy, sugary, or bland. If the student can more accurately describe the taste, you know if he or she prefers a chocolate bar to tart candies. To be a good communicator, exact vocabulary is important.

Getting to Know the Concept

Begin by talking about familiar words students frequently use. Explain that we can replace these words with more interesting words that show more clearly what we want to say. On a chart or board write the simple sentence, "My mom is sitting in a chair." Ask students to tell what kinds of chairs people sit in. Under the word *chair*, list their suggestions.

My mom is sitting in a **chair.**
> **recliner**
> **rocking chair**
> **bench**
> **kitchen chair**
> **computer chair**

To enlarge their vocabulary, you may want to add to the list with other suggestions, such as *chaise lounge, highchair, cane chair,* or *stool.* Discuss how replacing the word *chair* with one of the other words helps form a clearer picture in our minds. Explain that they can learn more interesting words from listening carefully to others and from reading.

Teaching the Concept With Literature

Reading aloud to students provides multiple opportunities to emphasize vocabulary words that are unusual or interesting. Point out examples where an author uses a word that is more vibrant than a familiar word students overuse. For example, when text says "she shouted," point out that instead of using *said* the author used *shouted* to give more meaning to the sentence. Select books that have colorful and unusual language. Use read-alouds as an opportunity to expand students' oral vocabulary.

Model Lesson

Build an "Interesting Words" word wall that shows each overused word and its interesting alternatives. Place a card with the overused word at the bottom of a ladder. Write at least three stronger synonyms on the upper rungs of the ladder.

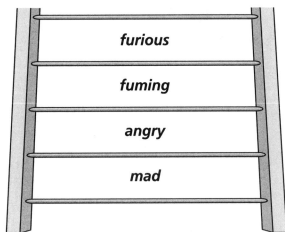

furious

fuming

angry

mad

Choose a book with interesting word choices, such as *How I Became a Pirate* (Long, 2003). This is the tale of a young boy who meets pirates on the beach, and becomes a pirate for one day. On the first page, Long writes, "I was at the beach building a sand castle. . . ." Using this sentence, pinpoint the author's use of the word *building* and write it on a word card. Ask students what they would say if they were building a sandcastle. If the word said is *making*, explain that this is an overused word, and write it on a card. Help students generate other words that could replace *building*, such as *constructing, creating, designing,* and *crafting.* Display the words in ladder formation so the more vibrant words are on the top rungs. On the second page, Long writes, "she was busy *slathering* my baby sister with sunblock." Repeat the activity with the word *slathering.* Follow this procedure with chosen words from the book, such as *shiver, announced, perfectly, pounded, gulped, commanded, swabbing, bellowed, confused,* and *noticed.* Continue to add to the "Interesting Words" word wall as you read other stories.

For additional practice, have each student complete an organizer at his or her skill level.

Graphic Organizers

Beginning: **Wonderful Words** (page 94) Students write three overused words from their reading and copy the sentence in which each word appears. They write more interesting words that could be used in place of the word.

Developing: **Boredom Buster** (page 95) Students write two overused words from their reading and copy the sentence in which each word appears. They write two or three other words or phrases to replace the basic word. Then they choose a replacement word and rewrite the sentence.

Extending: Charting **Ladder Leaps** (page 96)

Students write three overused words from their reading and copy the sentence in which each word appears. They then brainstorm words that can replace the overused word. They write three replacement words on the ladder in order from strong to strongest.

Great Books for This Activity

Picture Books

Florczak, R. (2003). *Yikes!!!* New York: Blue Sky.

Long, M. (2003). *How I became a pirate.* San Diego: Harcourt.

Weston, T. (2003). *Hey, pancakes!* San Diego: Harcourt.

Chapter Book

MacLachan, P. (1985). *Sarah, plain and tall.* New York: Harper & Row.

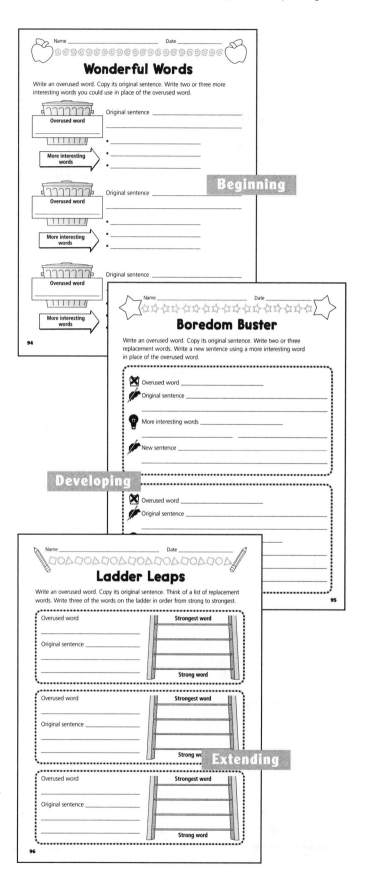

Wonderful Words

Write an overused word. Copy its original sentence. Write two or three more interesting words you could use in place of the overused word.

Overused word

_____

More interesting words

Original sentence _____

_____

• _____

• _____

• _____

Overused word

_____

More interesting words

Original sentence _____

_____

• _____

• _____

• _____

Overused word

_____

More interesting words

Original sentence _____

_____

• _____

• _____

• _____

Boredom Buster

Write an overused word. Copy its original sentence. Write two or three replacement words. Write a new sentence using a more interesting word in place of the overused word.

Overused word _____

Original sentence _____

_____

More interesting words _____

_____ _____

New sentence _____

_____

Overused word _____

Original sentence _____

_____

More interesting words _____

_____ _____

New sentence _____

_____

95

Ladder Leaps

Write an overused word. Copy its original sentence. Think of a list of replacement words. Write three of the words on the ladder in order from strong to strongest.

Overused word

_____

Original sentence _____

_____

_____

Strongest word

Strong word

Overused word

_____

Original sentence _____

_____

_____

Strongest word

Strong word

Overused word

_____

Original sentence _____

_____

_____

Strongest word

Strong word